Table of Contents

List of Figures

List of Tables

DYNAMIC BAYESIAN NETWORKS AS A PROBABILISTIC METAMODEL FOR COMBAT SIMULATION

I. Introduction

1.1 Background

Operations Research (OR) analysts as well as the Modeling and Simulation (M&S) community in general have adopted the saying by George Box that "all models are wrong, some are useful." This statement emphasizes the use of models for insight, not for perfect prediction. Models are wrong for a variety of reasons. Models are abstractions of reality and therefore necessarily incomplete. Since the models are necessarily incomplete, models cannot be fully validated. Models are based on assumptions associated with the reality they are meant to represent and these assumptions can be tenuous. Regardless of their fundamental incorrectness, models serve a useful purpose in providing a mechanism for the analyst to gain insight into the complexity of systems under study and ultimately support the decision-making process.

Gaining insight via a model-based analytical methodology requires the model be useful. In some circles, these useful models are validated for the purpose of the model use. But what exactly is meant by a useful model? In determining a model's usefulness, the first question to ask is whether or not the model is accurate? Though the model does not have to represent the entire system, it should not contain any inaccuracies, false assumptions or processes that do not exist in the real world system. The next concern should be the insight provided by the model. Does the model produce reasonable and useful answers or offer insight into addressing a specific question of the customer or leadership? Can statistically significant information, concerning a specific system, be gleaned from the model output? Can the model provide any predictions or inferences concerning the real world system represented? The efficiency of the model should be questioned? Does the model provide insightful answers in a reasonable amount of time and resources? If an answer is needed in two days, but the model takes a week to set up and run then the model is of no use. Also, is the model produced the quickest, cheapest or simplest model available? Finally, how useful is the model in providing insight into questions just outside the scope of the model? If there is another model available that runs faster, requires less memory and is easier to understand and implement, why not use what is already available? All of these questions should be considered when developing any model.

An important aspect of usefulness associated with any model, particularly those used in defense analysis, is how the model incorporates uncertainty. A deterministic model is defined as a model free of random elements; the model will produce the same results for a set of inputs. A stochastic model is defined as a model that includes random elements; the model output will vary each time for some set of inputs. Due to the uncertainty of the real world, analysts often prefer to capture that uncertainty using a stochastic model. The analytical challenge is that the output of a stochastic model is a random variable, a single observation from some population of possible observations. Thus, multiple replications of the model are required to develop the appropriate statistical measures of the model output and to be able to generate risk bounds (e.g., confidence intervals) around model outputs. In defense modeling, this approach to bounding the uncertainty is often referred to as Monte Carlo-based modeling.

Meriam-Webster defines uncertain as "Not reliable, not known, not clearly identified or defined or not constant." [33] In modeling terms, this means there are aspects of the model that are not accurately captured because there is variability of how those components of the reality modeled actually occur. The process of embedding this uncertainty in any model involves defining a probability distribution for each of the variable components in the reality and sampling from that distribution within the model. Each model run involves a *draw* from the appropriate probability distribution used by the model to generate some possible instance of reality. Multiple model runs yield separate independent draws from the probability distributions producing independent observations from the model. It is these independent observations that are the random variables the analyst must accommodate within their analysis.

Depending upon the size and complexity of the model, it may become impractical to run the model enough to generate the sample size required to gain the statistically valid risk bounds needed for the analysis. A simple answer to the problem might be to simply run the model deterministically by disabling the probability distributions and then using the collective of the distributions to place appropriate risk bounds on the model output. Since the deterministic model generally uses the expected values from each of the disabled probability distributions, the collective model output will represent the expected value of the model output as an estimate of the expected value of the reality being modeled. Placing risk bounds around this expected value is necessary and a the goal of this research.

Complex models can take a long time to run, even longer to sufficiently replicate. Some decision situations do not provide sufficient time to run these models to directly answer various questions posed. Since an analyst does not know these specific questions prior to their being asked, the analyst will not have the required results immediately available.

What the analyst can anticipate is the range of model values that will cover future questions. The analyst can thus run sufficient cases before-hand to characterize the range of model results. That characterization can be used to generate a very good estimate of the model response to inputs corresponding to a specific question.

Metamodeling is the term used to describe the response characterization. Regression modeling and neural networks are common metamodeling approaches. These approaches provide expected value results, but do a nice job of characterizing the response space based on the sampling of the full design space.

A metamodel that provides probabilistic estimates in addition to sufficient characterization of the sample space would be beneficial. The Dynamic Bayesian Network (DBN) has been proposed as a metamodeling method that captures the uncertainty and time element of the underlying model. There are issues associated with using the DBN, some of which are answered by this reseaerch.

1.1.1   Combat Modeling.

A discussion of modeling and simulation as it applies to military operations is useful. In 1811, Prussian war counselor, Baron von Reisswitz, developed, "Kriegsspiel" which was at the time the most creative and functional wargame the world had ever seen. Reisswitz's game can be referred to as the beginning of wargaming, or combat modeling, as a formal military analytical tool or area of study, [3], though abstract strategic force-on-force games date back to before 3000 B.C. [60] The exact birth of combat modeling is uncertain. Caffrey offers a thorough history of wargaming in his work *Toward a History-Based Doctrine for Wargaming* [3]. With the introduction of computers, warfare modeling transitioned from table-top efforts using topological maps to computer simulations, although human adjudication of outcomes are still used. These simulations rapidly evolved into complex programs capable of modeling numerous aspects of combat. Military models continue to improve and expand to include space elements, irregular warfare (IW) and even cyber scenarios. Today, the study of combat modeling and simulation includes everything from Computational Fluid Dynamics in weapon systems design to force-on-force engagement and campaign-level models of the operational systems. Figure 1 provides a concise outline of the standard combat modeling hierarchy. Note that the two lower levels in Figure 1

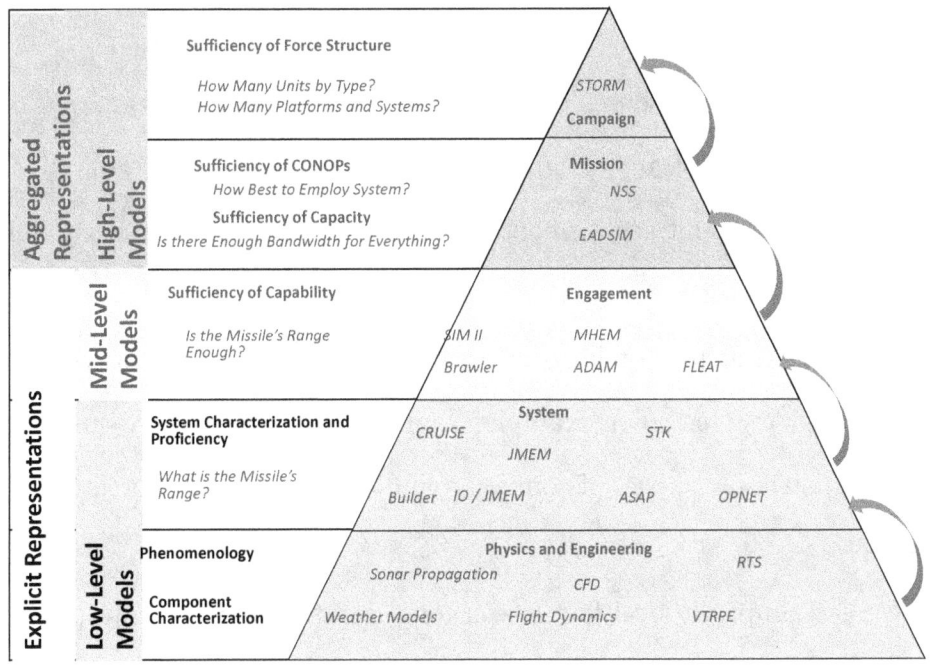

Figure 1. Combat Modeling Hierarchy [17]

are often combined into a single level labeled engineering.

The model hierarchy was created to depict changes in model focus as well as managerial use of those models. As one moves up the hierarchy, the models in each level decrease in the fidelity of each system component model. Alternatively , as one moves up the hierarchy, managerial involvement changes from the bench scientist at the lowest level to decision makers at the upper level.

At the lowest level, models are generally focused on system or system component design. Scientists and engineers focus on the definition and building of the system or system component as the primary uses.

The second level, System, involves models focused primarily on that system depicting how that system would function. For instance a missile under development may be *flown out* using a model slotted into this level.

The top three levels focus on operational use of the system; a well-engineered system must be operationally useful for it to be deployed and used.

The Engagement level focuses on short-duration operational scenarios involving relatively few systems, typically of similar function. For example, a radar system may be employed in an air-to-air engagement to assess its usefulness in finding, fixing, and helping to eliminate hostile targets.

The Mission level focuses on longer-duration (hours in length) involving relatively few collaborating systems. For example, a minimum level scenario may involve a flight of aircraft striking a series of command and control targets protected by ground defense systems.

Finally, the Campaign level focuses on long duration battles (days, weeks, etc). For example, a campaign level scenario may involve the whole-scale invasion of a country or territory involving systems from each of the participating services.

1.2 Problem Statement

The Department of Defense (DoD) needs to prepare for all kinds of attacks including cyber, terrorist, guerrilla, World War III and space, however, it funds only one force structure. The question that the DoD must answer is what is the optimal, or robust, force structure for the United States to effectively react to each campaign scenario or some subset of scenarios? AF/A9 is attempting to develop a process to answer such questions. The resulting AF/A9 project is called the Bayesian Enterprise Analysis Model (BEAM) which seeks to develop a new type of military modeling approach, one situated above campaign models in terms of aggregation. The BEAM type of model would provide a new top layer of the hierarchy depicted in Figure 1. Within this new layer, BEAM will provide a suite of tools for the DoD to evaluate defense force structures across multiple diverse campaign scenarios, account for the effects of new technology and account for enemy strategy changes or unexpected deviation.

The BEAM analytical process begins by first deciding what future planning scenarios the DoD should prepare for. Next, the resources, technology and strategies of the US, coalition partners and adversaries are researched and used as input in existing or new various low, mid and high level combat models to determine the results of various campaigns. Finally, the results of the models and uncertainty surrounding them are analyzed and a robust force structure is determined based on performance measures from each campaign model [17]. The metamodel for this project is best understood using Figures 2 and 3. Figure 2 depicts the modeling strategy for a single campaign. Based on variables such as Unit Types, Platforms, Weapons and Prioritization of Effort, strategies for the Blue and Red forces are determined. The effectiveness of each force is then determined based upon these variables, strategies and effectiveness of the opposing force. As the conflict continues, variables are updated, new strategies created and force effectiveness recalculated. Surrounding the entire campaign model is a level of uncertainty. Given each set of input variables into the campaign model there is some risk of implementing a specific strategy with uncertainty intervals about the expected performance of that strategy. In Figure 3 limitations on force structure are determined from constraints such as technology and funding. Next, the effectiveness and risk of different force structures across each cam-

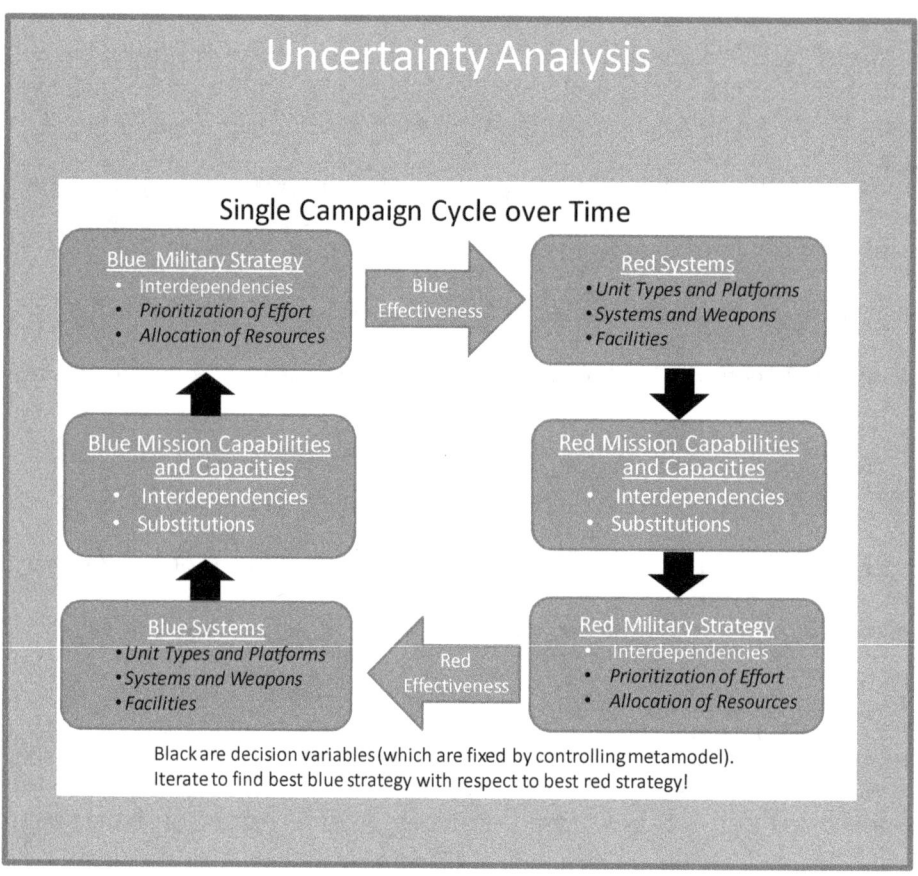

Figure 2. Campaign Model [17]

paign are analyzed to provide insight in determining a robust force structure. The Uncertainty Analysis (green boxes) shown in Figure 2 are a focus of this dissertation research.

The question of uncertainty or "fog of war" is an integral part in the defense modeling and simulation process. How uncertain are the results or what level of confidence can be placed on the results? Due to the increase in computer power, the standard approach to dealing with uncertainty is Monte Carlo simulation. For a stochastic model, simply run the model a sufficient number of times at various design points, based on some experimental design and then calculate confidence intervals based on the simulation estimates of variance. The problem with this method is

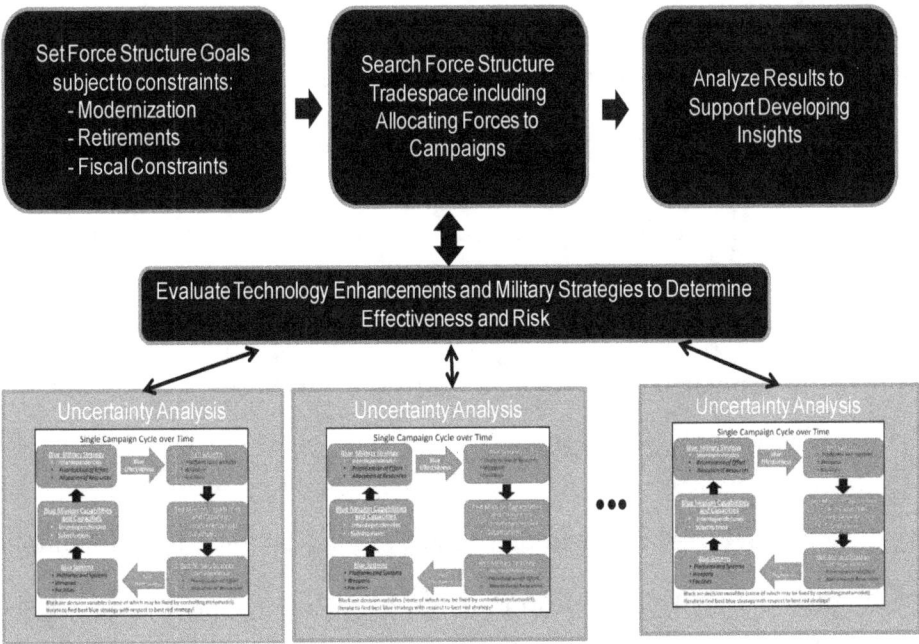

Figure 3. Multiple Campaign Metamodel [17]

that as the models get larger and become more complex simulation iterations become slower and more expensive. If an answer on force structure for the entire United States military is needed quickly, the Monte Carlo approach may not be practical for the complex combat models being used. Since the goal of BEAM is to optimize US force structure to prepare for multiple diverse campaign scenarios, some method other than Monte Carlo runs is needed to develop risk or uncertainty statements about the results. The research explores this idea of alternate uncertainty methods in combat modeling and simulation. The focus is on the use of Bayesian Networks (BN) and in particular DBNs as a means to encapsulate the campaign level meta-models. Specifically, the work extends current research in arguing for the use of DBNs as metamodels in the M&S world and validating their practicality.

1.3 Research Results

This research provides specific methodological improvements to make the DBN a viable combat model metamodeling approach. Specifically, this research

- defines and demonstrates the viability of bootstrapping to reduce model replications.

- Improves interpolation methods so that the DBN can be effectively used to characterize the response surface.

- Extends the DBN metamodeling approach from a single dimensional metamodel to a metamodel for the full response surface utilizing space filling designs.

- Demonstrates the methodlogy using an actual defense combat model.

1.4 Dissertation Overview

This dissertation is laid out in a journal paper compilation format. Chapter 2 presents the probabilistic modeling and analytical framework development to place the research into the context of simulation modeling and defense analysis. Chapter 3 provides the background necessary to understand BNs and DBNs. Chapter 4 extends the bootstrapping method from re-sampling individual responses to re-sampling simulation runs and demonstrates the use of bootstrapping to improve the efficiency of building a DBN metamodel. Chapter 5 extends the DBN metamodel method to characterize full response spaces and presents a new, much improved interpolation method by which one can use the DBN to provide estimates anywhere in the design space. Chapter 6 presents a defense model case study demonstrating the viability of using the DBN for defense analytical metamodeling. Finally a summary of the research and final comments are provided in Chapter 7.

II. An Analytical Framework

2.1 Frameworks

A framework is defined as "a basic conceptional structure (as of ideas)" or "a skeletal, openwork, or structural frame." [33] It is a guide or conceptual model that helps to define the hierarchy, levels or structure of a particular process or system. Some examples of frameworks are an educational framework that maps out the rules, standards and progression of learning in an educational system or a software framework that provides the basic skeleton for some product which can be manipulated or improved by different users. There are a variety of frameworks available and these vary in terms of their technical detail and purpose. In this section, two frameworks, useful for this dissertation, are discussed.

2.1.1 Modeling Framework.

A modeling framework is an abstraction of the modeling process. Modeling is quite an ambiguous term as it can range from some human entertainment activity to the intellectual activity of building a theoretical representation of some naturally occurring system. For purposes of this research, Defense Modeling, the focus is on the process of defining, designing, building, testing and executing some computational model. These models include simulation models, queuing models and optimization models. Each of these models may be deterministic or stochastic.

A general outline of the simulation modeling process is found in a conference paper by Withers et al. [64] and is presented below. The authors depict their simulation modeling framework using the Integrated Definition (IDEF) activity modeling methodology, $IDEF\varnothing$.

11

1. UNDERSTAND THE SYSTEM AND CUSTOMER. In this step, the customer and modeler will discuss the system to be modeled clearly defining the resources, constraints, objectives and questions to be answered. This will eventually help to define and scope those system aspects that will be modeled.

2. PRODUCE CONCEPTUAL MODEL. In this step, the modeler, based on guidance from the customer, produces a conceptual model. This conceptual model could take the form of a flow chart, a diagram such as a value-stream map or unified modeling language description, or some other method of conceptualizing the system to be modeled. This step helps to ensure that the modeler and customer are in agreement of what constitutes the abstract representation of the system of interest.

3. PRODUCE MODEL. This step is where the coding and mathematics occur. Typical questions to answer during this step include:

   - Will the model be deterministic or stochastic?

   - Will the model be continuous time or discrete time?

   - Will the model be consolidated or exploratory in nature?

   - What inputs will be needed and where does the data come from?

   - What outputs are needed and will be generated by the model?

   - What level of model validation will be required to ensure the model is useful?

4. USE MODEL. This step involves how the analyst will employ the model to answer questions posed by their customers or leadership. It might also include pre-planned improvements to the model to accommodate its expanded use. De-

vices like use-cases might be generated to provide a template for how to employ the model for analytical purposes.

5. ASSESS MODEL USE. In this final step, the model is used to assist analysis and help analysts produce insights to answer questions regarding the reality represented by the model.

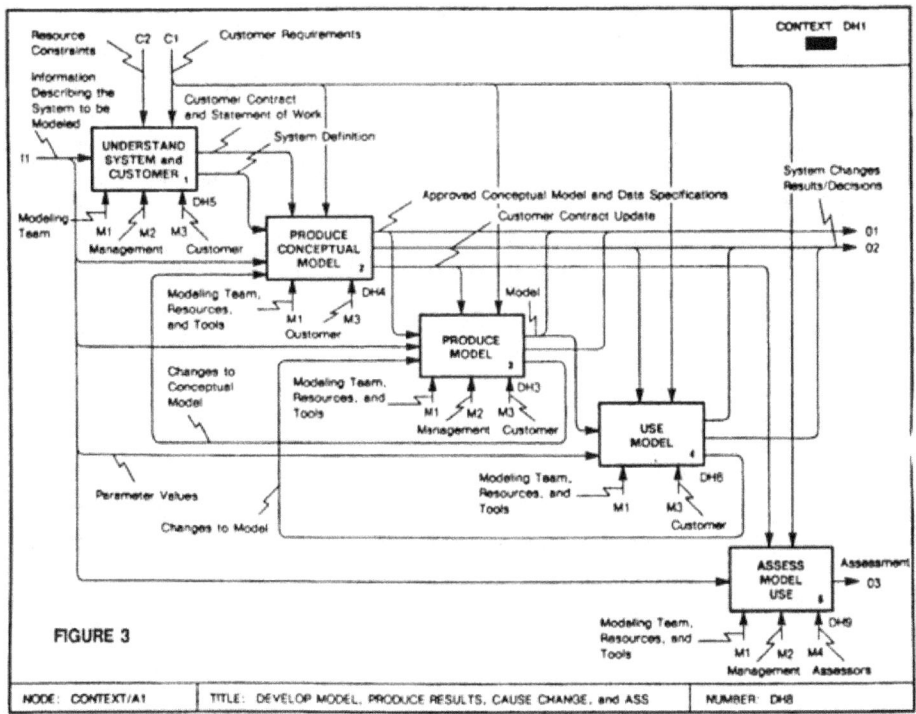

Figure 4. Summary of IDEF0 Steps [64]

Figure 4 depicts the high-level steps outlined in Withers et al [64]. Each node in Figure 4 has its sub IDEF0 so that the whole framework is a set of models or IDEF0s with sub models. Figure 5 depicts the sub-IDEF0 for step 3, PRODUCE MODEL. Changes can be made to the five steps presented in Figure 5. Some of the questions in step 3 can be answered in step 2. The improvement runs in step 4 may be done in step 3. Regardless of what changes may or may not be made, this work is a good first step in defining a general framework for modeling. Certain standards and rules are

13

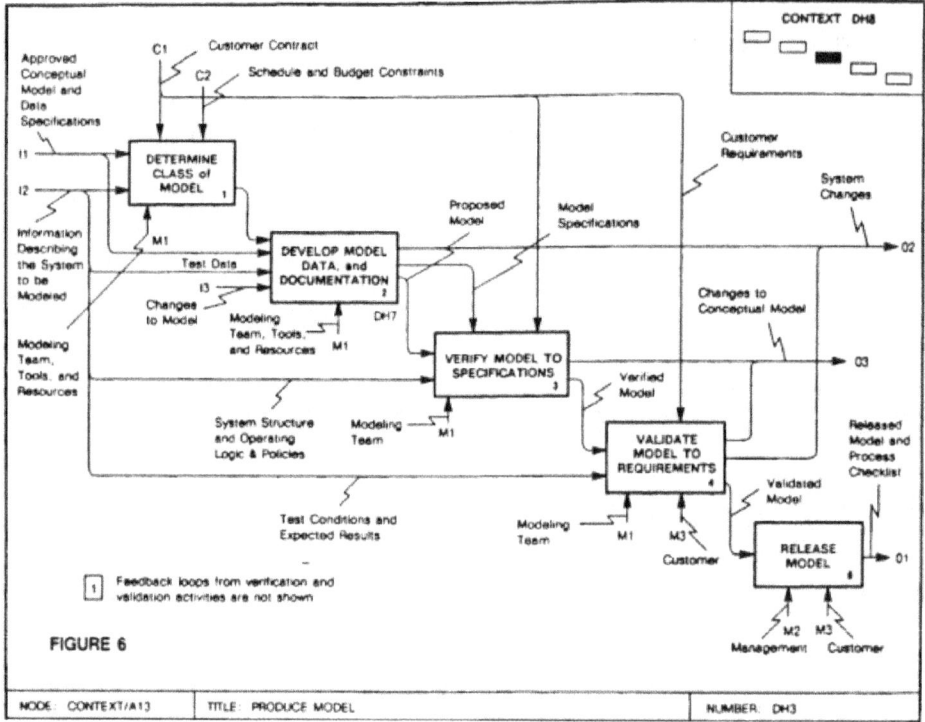

Figure 5. IDEF0 for Step 3 [64]

used in frameworks requiring the models be well documented, easily understood and the code easily implementable from one customer to another. Seila [56] argues that since certain industry standards were developed for architecture so each architect can easily understand the others drawings, there should be a set of standards for model description. Seila proposes four simple options that every modeling system should allow the user to do [56]:

- Specify the model;

- Visualize the model;

- Construct the simulation program; and

- Document the system, model and simulation program.

14

These options above are only available to the user if there is some universal standard for modeling and simulation. Davis outlines numerous attributes that should be evident in all military models, a few of which are listed here [9]:

- Models should be consistent with and reinforce the principles of war.

- Overall modeling activity should not be dominated by any one approach (i.e., neither the "bottom up" nor the "top down" approaches are "right")

- Models should reflect stochastic effects, at least optionally. Further, deterministic operations should be based on results of stochastic modeling. This may require distinguishing among cases rather than settling on expected-value calculations, because outcome distributions are so often skewed and multimodal

- Adaptive strategies and tactics should be emphasized; scripted strategies and tactics should be avoided, since they teach stereotypes and encourage complacency.

- The traditional distinction between gaming and closed simulation is obsolete. Models for analysis often need to be interruptible and flexible. Also, a gaming style of analysis is often quite valuable.

Though no universal definition of a Modeling Framework exists, developing a framework based on IDEF0 models with certain standards and rules will make the model for any research project easy to produce and in turn easy to interpret and implement.

2.1.2 Analytical Framework.

Based on research to date, there does not appear to be any set or understood analytical framework for the realm of modeling and simulation. First, what is meant by analytical? It could refer to the construction of the analytical portion of the model. For example how do the variables interact mathematically within the processes of the model? Analytical could also refer to the analysis of the output such as sensitivity analysis or confidence intervals on output responses. For the frameworks, analytical refers to the activities involved in the scope of a particular study.

An activity diagram represents the activities taken as a snapshot. It is not a diagram that involves time or process. As such an activity diagram abstracts out many of the details one finds when examining an activity. The purpose of the Analytical Framework is to describe the process of analysis, in a general sense, as from the perspective of an analyst (versus a manager or decision maker). At this point, a general Analytical Framework is proposed for the researcher using the IDEF0 method as used in Withers et al [64].

To create the Analytical Framework, multiple analysts with real world experience were interviewed. Each analyst had worked on different projects and therefore had different views, processes, opinions and issues to bring to the table. One of the major problems that arises in almost every analysis is gathering data. Either it is too expensive to gather all the data necessary to perform the analysis or data has been collected, but it needs to be cleaned up or is completely useless. It is important that the analyst be involved in the experimentation and data gathering process of the project so that useful data is collected efficiently.

A second issue is clearly defining the problem statement. Before launching into any analysis a rigorous understanding of the question at hand is necessary. This second issue leads into the next problem and that is the inexperience or lack of education in Statistics and Operations Research among many of the analysts. Many analysts do not have the tool set or knowledge to ask the right questions and end up running some program that has always been run using templates to understand the output,

16

with no ability to explore the problem and discover a more sophisticated, creative and often better solution.

The interviews pointed out that a common problem in the analysis process that cannot be remedied through a framework is the relationship between the analyst and decision maker. The analyst must have the skill to question and extract the correct problem statement from the decision maker and then the communication abilities necessary to present the results both intermediate during a study and final results at the end of a study. At the same time the decision maker needs a basic knowledge of analysis to understand the results and must be willing to listen to and consider the analysis even if the results conflict with their experienced view.

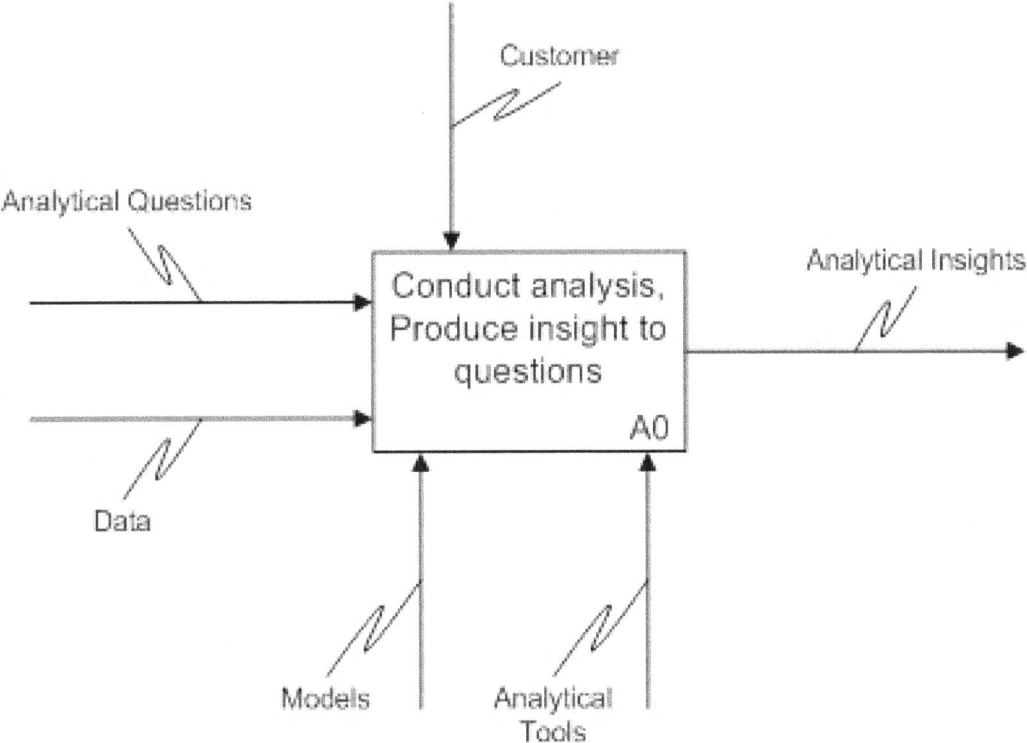

Figure 6. *A∅* **level diagram of Analytical Framework**

Figure 6 presents the *A∅* level diagram, a top-level view of analysis. The analytical process takes as input the Analytical Questions posed, and supporting Data

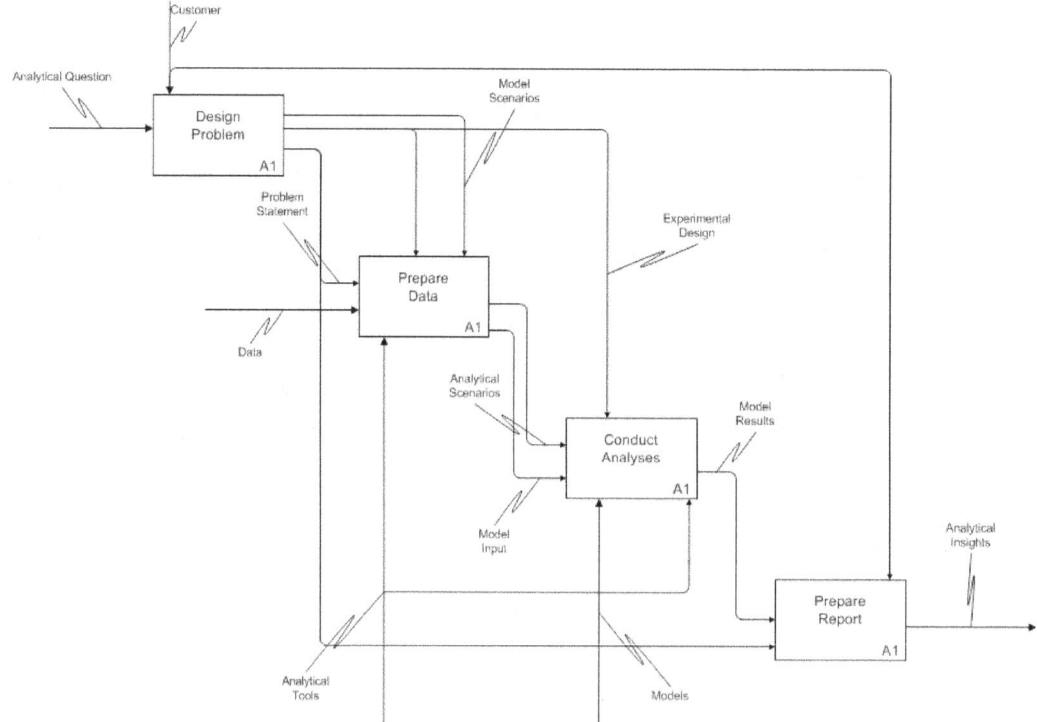

Figure 7. *A*1 **level diagram of Analytical Framework**

to generate the requested Analytical Insights. These efforts are controlled by the Customer while Models and various Analytical Tools are the mechanism by which the analyst completes the analytical activity.

Figure 7 is the first-level decomposition. During the conduct of the analysis, the analyst finds four activities. First is defining the exact problem to generate the actionable Problem Statement. Coupled with this will be the specific Model Scenarios with Experimental Design used to scope how to prepare the data and run the models.

The Prepare Data activity in Figure 7 converts the Data obtained from various sources into the form needed to conduct the analyses (whether or not the analyses are model-based). The final forms of the data are controlled by the model scenarios and experimental design and are achieved using appropriate Analytical Tools as the data preparation mechanism.

18

The suite of Analytical Tools then serve as the mechanism to convert the Analytic Scenarios and Model Input into the derived Model Results.

Finally, the analyst generates the Analytical Insight in the Prepare Report activity which converts the Problem Statement and supporting Model Results into the insight required under the control of the study Customer.

The Analytical Framework puts into context research conducted for the analyst. Much of the operational research-focus is on the Analytical Tools mechanism. For the current research, the focus is how to provide a metamodeling approach (new analytical tool) that yields probabilistic (versus deterministic) output.

2.1.3 Probabilistic Modeling.

Uncertainty is inherent in all systems. Models often need to capture their modeled system uncertainty. Currently, the main approach for incorporating uncertainty into a model is via Monte Carlo simulation. However, other ways include Bayesian Networks (BN), Decision Trees and Game Theory; each help in understanding uncertainty and modeling in a multi-scenario situation. Halpern in his book *Reasoning About Uncertainty* [19] refers to multiple methods of dealing with uncertainty including Dempster-Schafer Belief Functions, Ranking Functions, Plausibility measures and Modal Logic. There are obviously many ways of explaining uncertainty, but are they useful for modeling and simulation and if so how can they be utilized?

Our focus will be BNs, which when expanded to model the time component are called Dynamic Bayesian Networks (DBN). Combat models generally employ Monte Carlo methods to model uncertainty. Our use of the DBN will be as a metamodel of various stochastic combat model runs. This research establishes improved ways to conduct military-focused metamodeling to explicitly capture the probabilistic aspects of modeling.

III. Bayesian Networks

3.1 Bayesian Networks

A Bayesian Network (BN) is a directed acyclic graph (DAG) that describes the causal relationship between several random variables through joint probability distributions [47]. Bayesian Belief Networks, Belief Networks, Causal Networks, Probability Networks, and DAG models are other names that appear in the literature [8], however, the popular use of the term Bayesian Networks is attributed to Judea Pearl in his work, *Bayesian Networks: a model of self-activated memory for evidential reasoning* [8] [41]. While, it may be a stretch to say that Pearl is the father of BNs due to the parallel work done at the time, his work in the 1980s is often cited as its formal beginning. There are traces of BNs, or similar methods, in use as early as the 1920s. In 1923 and later in 1934 Sewall Wright, produced two major papers on path analysis in studying genetic inheritance [65] [66] [50] and later in 1963 Marvin Minsky mentions *Baye's Nets* in his work on artificial intelligence [36] [21].

3.1.1 Definition.

A formal definition of Bayesian Networks from Jensen and Nielsen's book, *Bayesian Networks and Decision Graphs* [21], is presented:

Definition 3.1.1 *A* Bayesian Network *consists of the following:*

- *A set of variables and a set of* directed edges *between variables*

- *Each variable has a finite set of mutually exclusive states.*

- *The variables together with the directed edges form an* acyclic directed graph *(traditionally abbreviated DAG); a directed graph is* acyclic *if there is no directed path* $A_1 \rightarrow ... \rightarrow A_n$ *so that* $A_1 = A_n$

20

- *To each variable A with parents $B_1, ..., B_n$, a conditional probability table $P(A|B_1, ..., B_n)$ is attached.*

A simple example is provided to illustrate the definition.

3.1.2 Example.

Suppose you are a doctor specializing in lung diseases and you need a quick method for diagnosing your patients based on their conditions. Your main concern consists of three major lung diseases: tuberculosis, lung cancer and bronchitis. After some research you are able to develop the BN depicted in Figure 8. Just to understand

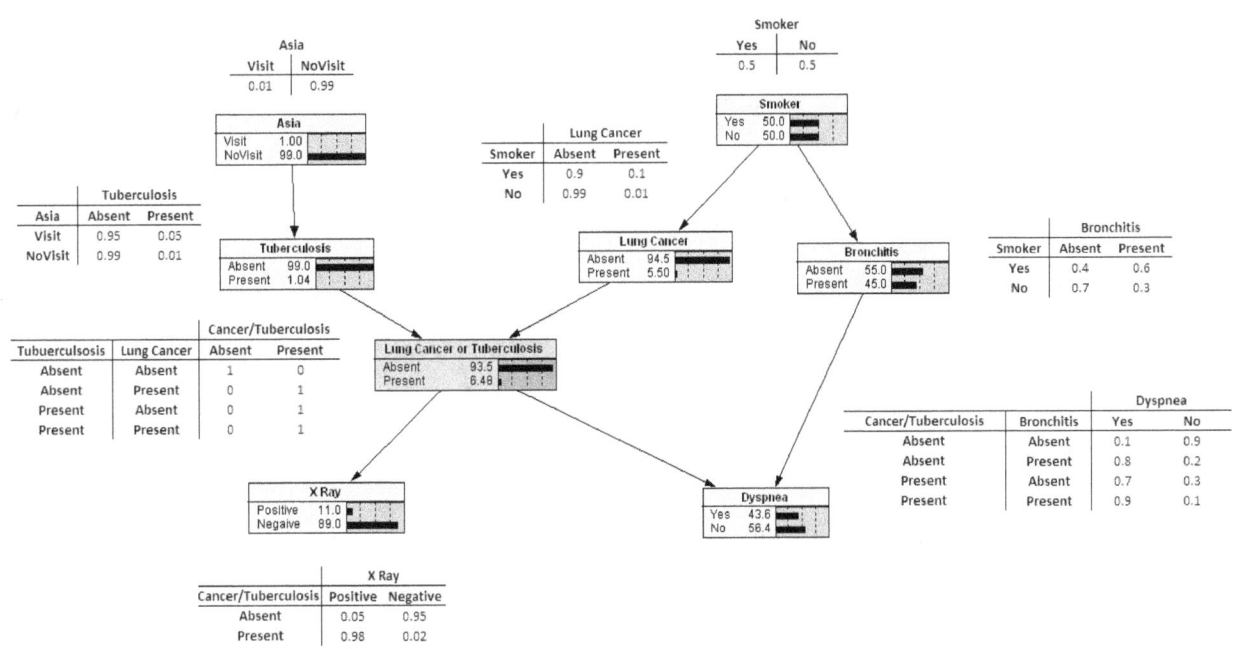

Figure 8. Medical Diagnostic Example

how the network works suppose you have a patient that has either lung cancer or tuberculosis, but definitely does not have bronchitis. What is the probability that this patient suffers from dyspnea (Difficult breathing). This example is not very realistic, but provided to show how the network is used. His network is now adjusted to account

21

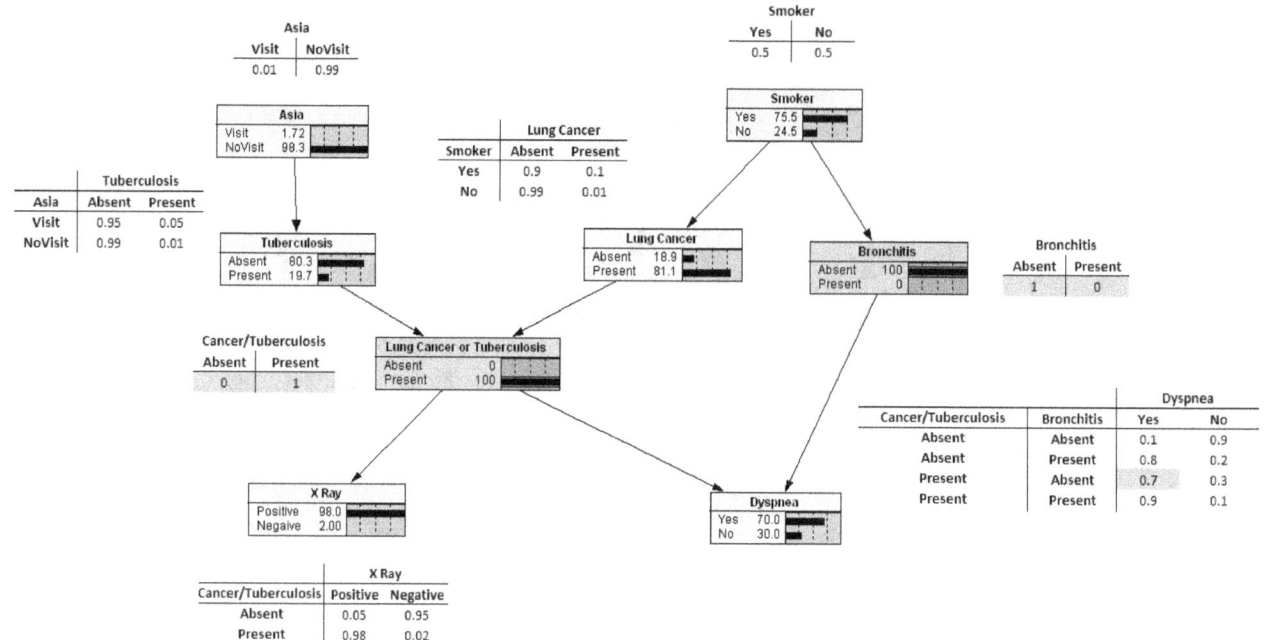

Figure 9. Medical Diagnostic Example P(Dyspnea—Cancer or Tuberculosis, No Bronchitis)

for this information or evidence. Notice that chances of the patient complaining of dyspnea have increased to 70% as is highlighted in Figure 9.

3.1.3 Properties.

After defining BNs, Jensen and Nielsen outline two basic properties of BNs that follow from their definition. Before presenting these properties, however, it is necessary to introduce the concept of d-separation, defined as follows [21]:

Definition 3.1.2 *Two distinct variables A and B in a causal network are* d-separated *("d" for "directed graph") if for all paths between A and B, there is an intermediate variable V (distinct from A and B) such that either*

- *the connection is serial or diverging and V is instantiated* [the state of the variable is known]*;*

  or

22

- *the connection is converging, and neither V nor any of V's descendants have received evidence* [instantiated].

If A and B are not d-separated, we call them d-connected.

To help in understanding, the medical diagnostic BN will be used to illustrate d-separation. There are three possible cases to consider: converging (multiple arcs converging to one node), diverging (multiple arcs coming out of one node) and serial (one arc entering a node is followed by another arc leaving that node). Each of these cases can be at looked in their simplest form involving only two arcs. Therefore case one will be referred to as the head-to-head case since the arcs meet at their heads, case two will be referred to as the tail-to-tail case since the arcs meet at their tails and the third case will be the head-to-tail case since the head of one arc meets the other at its tail. These terms were taken from Dr. Mahoney's lecture on Bayesian Networks and NETICA [32].

In Figure 10 those nodes which are d-connected to the node "Lung Cancer or Tuberculosis" are highlighted in orange. When "Lung Cancer or Tuberculosis" is instantiated with evidence, node "Lung Cancer" is now d-connected to "Tuberculosis" and nodes "Asia" and "X-Ray" are d-separated from them as is seen in Figure 11. This can be understood by simply thinking about how information is passed through the network. When "Lung Cancer or Tuberculosis" is not instantiated "Asia" and "Tuberculosis" are passing information to "X-Ray" in that visits to Asia can effect whether or not a patient gets tuberculosis which in turn effects the results of the X-Ray. However, when it is known the patient has either lung cancer or tuberculosis it doesn't matter whether or he/she visits Asia or gets tuberculosis the results of the X-Ray depend only on having a disease and do not distinguish between lung cancer or tuberculosis. Thus, in a Head-to-Tail connection evidence on the connecting node d-separates the connecting node's parent and child nodes.

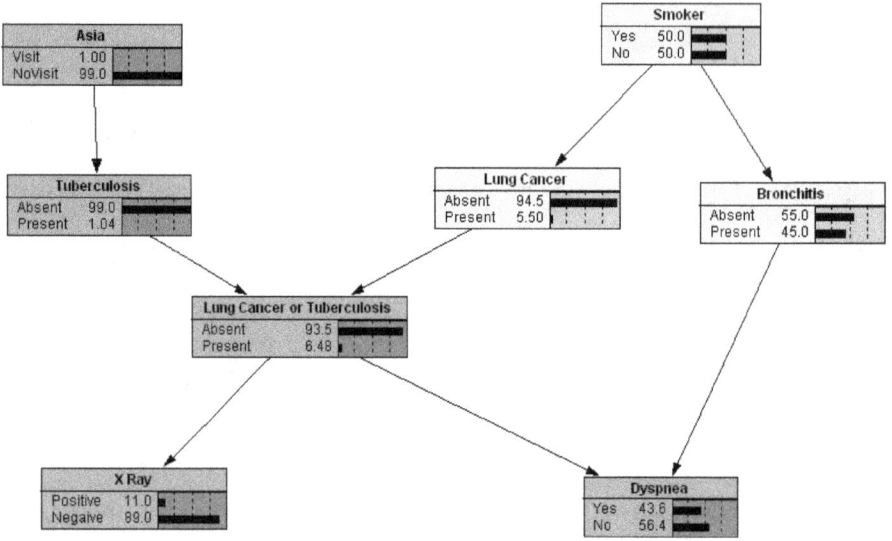

Figure 10. Medical Diagnostic d-Separation Example (Non-Instantiated)

For the Head-to-Head case it is clear from the figures that evidence on the connecting nodes d-connects its two parent nodes, but why? If you do not know whether a patient has tuberculosis or lung cancer then if the patient gets tuberculosis that should not effect his/her chances of getting lung cancer. However, if it is known that the patient has either lung cancer or tuberculosis then chances of having either one have increased. Suppose you determine the patient does not have lung cancer, it must be that the patient has tuberculosis and therefore information has been passed from "Lung Cancer" to "Tuberculosis" through the instantiated node "Lung Cancer or Tuberculosis."

Finally, what are the d-separation rules in the Tail-to-Tail case? Returning to Figure 8 where "Lung Cancer or Tuberculosis" has not been instantiated, it is evident that "X-Ray" is d-connected to "Dyspnea." Since you have no evidence concerning

24

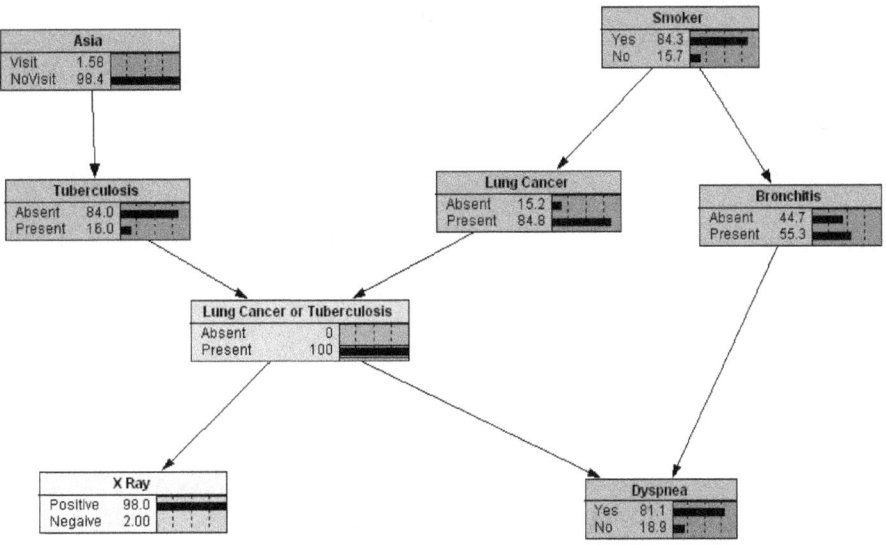

Figure 11. Medical Diagnostic d-Separation Example (Instantiated)

the patient's disease, if the patient complains of dyspnea this will increase their chance of a disease and in turn raise his/her chances of having a positive X-Ray which implies d-connection through the node "Lung Cancer or Tuberculosis". Now, suppose you know the patient has either Tuberculosis or Cancer. The X-rays only depend upon the disease of the patient and therefore having dyspnea will not effect the outcome of the X-Rays since a disease is already present and, vice versa, a positive X-Ray has no bearing on dyspnea since dyspnea is only a symptom of one of the diseases, which is already present. d-separation can be a complicated concept to grasp. For more examples see [32].

Having a better understanding of d-separation, Jensen and Nielsen's BN properties are [21]:

Bayesian Network Properties

Let $\mathcal{U} = \{A_1, ..., A_n\}$ be a universe of variables, BN be a Bayesian Network over $\mathcal{U}$ and $P(\mathcal{U})$ be a probability distribution reflecting the following properties:

    i the conditional probabilities for a variable given its parents in $P(\mathcal{U})$ must be as specified in BN, and

    ii if the variables A and B are d-separated in BN given the set $\mathcal{C}$, then A and B are independent given $\mathcal{C}$ in $P(\mathcal{U})$

Property two can be rewritten as follows:

    If A and B are d-separated in the BN given the set $\mathcal{C}$, then $P(A|B) = P(A)$ and $P(B|A) = P(B)$

Thus, through this concept of d-separation, BNs have a natural independence in their structure.

Next, the Chain Rule for Bayesian Networks is presented [21]:

Theorem 3.1.1 (The Chain Rule for Bayesian Networks) *Let BN be a Bayesian Network over $\mathcal{U} = \{A_1, ..., A_n\}$. Then BN specifies a unique joint probability distribution $P(\mathcal{U})$ given by the product of all conditional probability tables specified in BN:*

$$P(\mathcal{U}) = \prod_{i=1}^{n} P(A_i|pa(A_i)), \qquad (3.1)$$

where $pa(A_i)$ are the parents of A_i in BN, and $P(\mathcal{U})$ reflects the properties of BN

Theorem 3.1.1 follows from the fundamental rule for variables, $P(A \bigcap B) = P(A|B)P(B)$ or $P(A \bigcap B|C) = P(A|B \bigcap C)P(B|C)$ [21] and general chain rule of probability theory.

Using the Chain Rule and Bayes' Theorem the Bayesian Network can now be utilized to answer specific questions.

Returning to the diagnostic example, suppose you have a patient diagnosed with lung cancer. You are concerned about the patient getting bronchitis and therefore want to know the chance of bronchitis given lung cancer. Due to the structure of the BN and d-separation, the only variables of concern are bronchitis, lung cancer, smoking and dyspnea.

Let B, C, S and D represent the variables bronchitis, lung cancer, smoking and dyspnea respectively. Letters in small caps will be used to denote the state of each variable. For example, b_1 represents the patient having bronchitis and b_2 the patient not having bronchitis. The solution to this probability is a bit more complicated and requires the use of Bayes' Theorem.

$$P(B|A) = \frac{P(A|B)P(B)}{P(A)} = \frac{P(A \bigcap B)}{P(A)} \propto P(A \bigcap B) \qquad \text{(Bayes' Theorem)}$$

Note that $\propto$ implies that $P(B|A)$ is proportional to $P(A \bigcap B)$ by some constant. Since you are concerned about the chances of the patient having bronchitis, first find $P(b_1|c_1)$. (Note that each of the values used in this solution were taken from the

CPTs in Figure 8):

$$P(b_1|c_1) = \frac{P(b_1 \bigcap c_1)}{(c_1)}$$

$$= \alpha P(b_1 \bigcap c_1)$$

$$= \alpha \sum_{S,D} P(b_1 \bigcap S \bigcap c_1 \bigcap D)$$

$$= \alpha \sum_{S,D} P(S)P(c_1|S)P(b_1|S)P(D|b_1)$$

$$= \alpha[P(s_1)P(c_1|s_1)P(b_1|s_1) + P(s_2)P(c_1|s_2)P(b_1|s_2)][P(d_1|b_1) + P(d_2|b_1)]$$

$$= \alpha[P(s_1)P(c_1|s_1)P(b_1|s_1) + P(s_2)P(c_1|s_2)P(b_1|s_2)][1]$$

$$= \alpha[(0.5)(0.1)(0.6) + (0.5)(0.01)(0.3)][1]$$

$$= \alpha 0.0315$$

A similar procedure for b_2 yields $P(b_2|c_1) = \alpha 0.0235$. $P(b_1|c_1) + P(b_2|c_1) = 1$ implies that $\alpha = 18.18181$, $P(b_1|c_1) = 0.573$ and $P(b_2|c_1) = 0.427$. Thus, the patient with lung cancer now has a 57% chance of getting bronchitis as opposed to the original 45% chance without lung cancer. These results can be seen in the network in Figure 12 The case where exact knowledge is known and inputted into the network is called *hard evidence*. There are two other types of evidence which are defined below along with hard evidence. These definitions are taken from [28]

Definition 3.1.3 • A hard finding *is an* instantiation, $X_i = x_i^l$ *for a particular value of* $i \in 1, ...d$ *and a particular value of* $l \in 1, ..., k_i$. *This specifics that variable* X_i *is in the state* x_i^l. *It is expressed as a* $k_1 \times ... \times k_d$ *potential e where*

$$e(x_1^{(p_1)}, ..., x_d^{(p_d)}) = \begin{cases} 1 & p_i = l \\ 0 & p_i \neq l \end{cases} \tag{3.2}$$

28

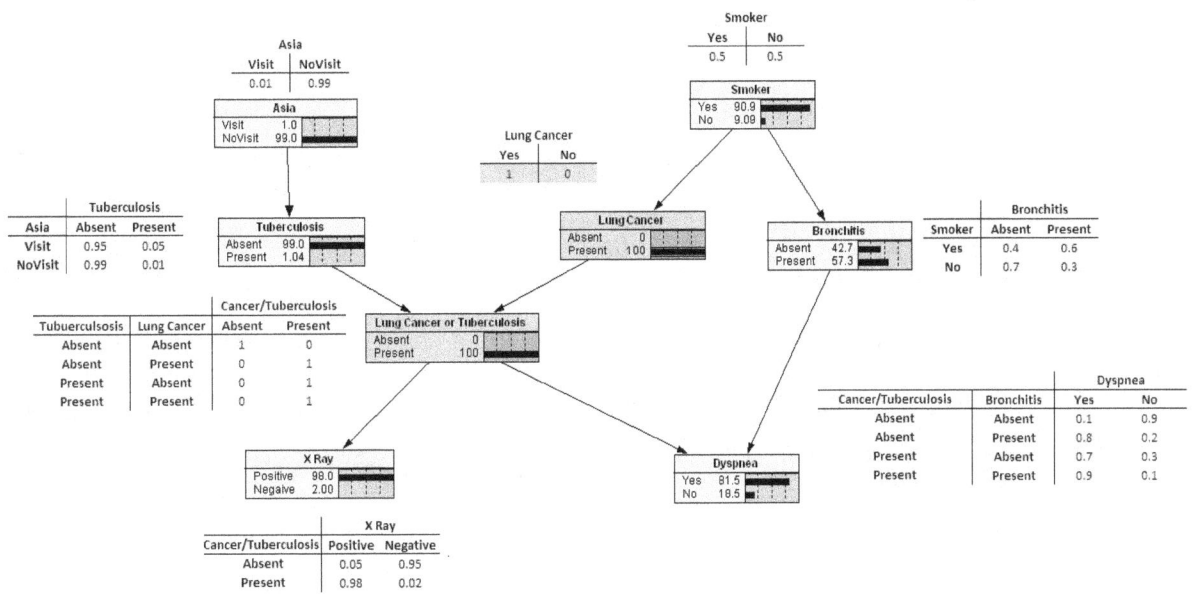

Figure 12. Medical Diagnostic Example $P(Bronchitis|LungCancer)$

*That is, the entries corresponding to configurations containing the instantiation
are 1 and the entries corresponding to all other configurations are 0.*

- Hard evidence *is a collection of hard findings. It is given by a collection of
  potentials* $e = (e_1, ..., e_m)$ *where* e_m *is a hard finding on one of the variables.*

- *A* Soft finding *on a variable* X_j *specifies the probability distribution of the vari-
  able* X_j. *That is, the potential* $p_{X_j|\Pi_j}$ *is replaced by a potential* $p^*_{X_j}$ *with domain*
  X_j.

29

- Soft evidence *is a collection of soft findings.*

- *A Virtual finding on variable X_j is a collection of likelihood ratios $L(x_j^{(m)})$, $m = 1, ..., m$ such that the updated conditional probability potential for $X_j|\Pi_j = \pi_j^n$ is, for $m = 1, ..., k_j$,*

$$p_{X_j|\Pi_j}^{*}(x_j^{(m)}|\pi_j^{(n)}) = \frac{1}{\Sigma_{q=1}^{k_j} p_{X_j|\Pi_j}(x_j^{(q)}|\pi_j^{(q)})L(x_j^{(q)})} p_{X_j|\Pi_j}(x_j^{(m)}|\pi_j^n)L(x_j^{(m)}) \quad (3.3)$$

- Virtual evidence *is a collection of virtual findings.*

Updating the network with hard evidence has already been illustrated, but what about the cases of soft and virtual evidence. Typically when soft evidence is received for some variable, say X, the potential or joint probability distribution for that variable is replaced with the new evidence and all parents of the variable X are disconnected since they no longer effect its states. However, Peng et al. [45] show how to translate soft evidence into virtual evidence, which does not require the disconnection of parents. Therefore this paper will only be concerned with propagating virtual evidence within a network. Pearl developed a method for updating a network with virtual evidence, which introduces the evidence into the network as a new node [28] and then instantiates that node to propagate the evidence through the network. Again using the medical BN from before, an example of inputting soft evidence, and in turn virtual evidence, into a work is demonstrated.

Suppose more recent data and research gives you reason to believe that the joint probability distribution for dyspnea is not correct. You believe that in reality only 30% of your patients suffer from dyspnea instead of the current 43.6% as seen in Figure 8. You would like to put this new distribution in for dyspnea without breaking the current network or changing the CPTs. Let D represent the variable dyspnea with d_1 and d_2 signifying the patient complains of dyspnea or not respectively. The current joint probability distribution for D is $P(D) = (P(d_1), P(d_2)) = (43.6\%, 56.4\%)$, but you would like to change this to $(30\%, 70\%)$. First the soft evidence needs to be changed to virtual evidence. To put it another way, the probability distribution you want to enter as evidence needs to be transformed into likelihood ratios. This is accomplished by taking the desired probabilities and dividing them by the current probabilities. Thus, the likelihood ratios for dyspnea, denoted λ_D, are $\lambda_D = (0.3/0.436 : 0.7/0.564) = (0.688 : 1.241)$. The ratios are then normalized yielding the distribution $(35.6\%, 64.4\%)$. To introduce the virtual evidence into the network a new node, V is created and connected to the network as a child node of dyspnea. Node V has two states: $v_1 = dyspnea\ present$ and $v_2 = dyspnea\ absent$. The distribution from the normalized likelihood ratios is used to parameterize the CPT of the virtual node. These steps are summarized in the BN in Figure 13. Finally, to input the soft evidence into the network, node V must be instantiated with the evidence that $P(v_1 = 1)$. This evidence can be propagated through the network as hard evidence now. The results are shown in Figure 14. As Figure 14 shows, the soft evidence is now incorporated into the dyspnea node.

This method for propagating virtual evidence was derived by Pearl and can be further studied in [45] [28].

Updating or propagating evidence through a network, can become very difficult especially for larger networks. Fortunately, different methods and algorithms have been developed to expedite this process. The two standard approaches are propagation via junction trees and stochastic simulation. Belief propagation through junction trees or stochastic simulation is too long a process to describe here. However, Neapolitan's work [39] proved very useful in understanding the junction tree algorithms and actually provided a concrete example using the medical diagnostic network this paper has repeatedly referenced. Jensen [21] offers a good overview of stochastic simulation

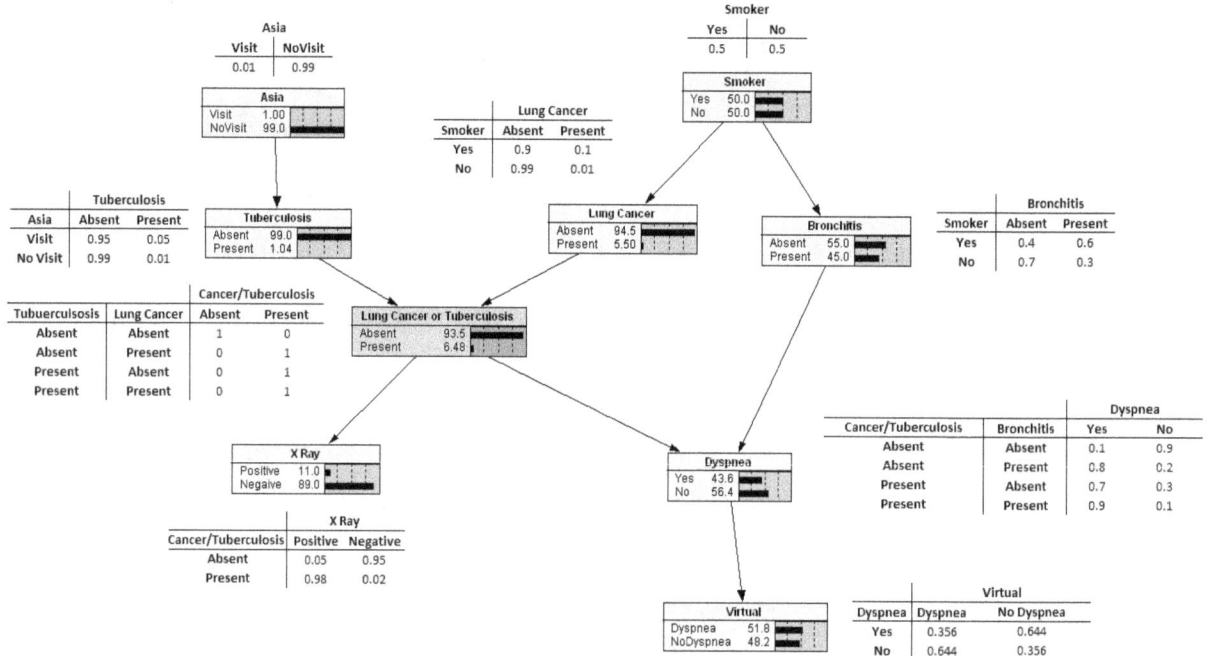

Figure 13. Medical Diagnostic Soft Evidence Example (Non-Instantiated)

and the major algorithms used: probabilistic logic sampling, likelihood weighting and Gibbs sampling. While this is not an exhaustive list of the techniques available, the resources provided are a good starting point in determining an optimal method of belief updating.

Up to this point no distinction has been made between discrete or continuous variables in a BN. Nodes in a BN are typically treated as discrete and therefore continuous variables must be discretized. This issue of discretization is not addressed in the research; however, Uusitalo [62] offers some discussion on the matter and

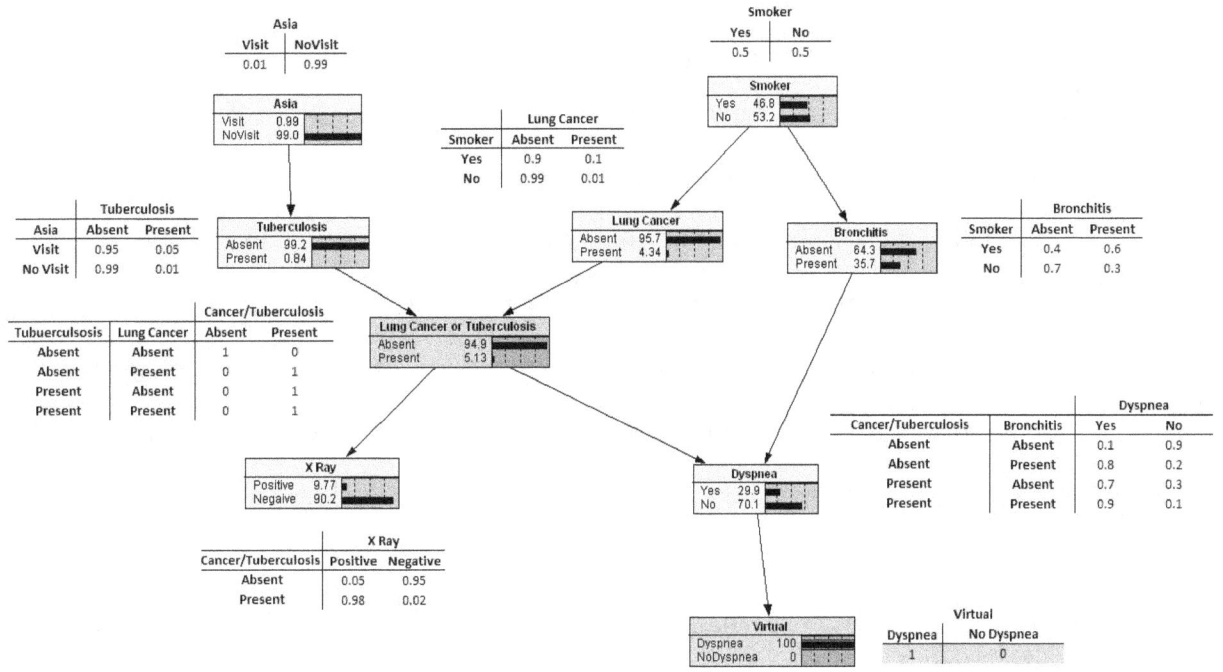

Figure 14. Medical Diagnostic Soft Evidence Example (Instantiated)

provides various references for further study. Some theory has been developed to handle continuous nodes in BN using linear conditional Gaussian distributions.

Assuming Gaussian distributions on all continuous nodes in some Bayesian Network, BN, consider node X with some set of parent nodes. Let $paX = \{paX_1, ..., paX_m\}$ denote the set of continuous parents of X and the constant σ_x^2 the variance of the Gaussian distribution on X independent of paX. Then the mean of X, μ_x, can be written as a linear combination of the means of its continuous parents:

$$\mu_x = \beta_0 + \sum_{i=1}^{m} \mu_{paX_i} \tag{3.4}$$

Note that *hybrid Bayesian Networks*, BNs containing both continuous and discrete variables, can exist, but typically discrete variables can not have continuous parents; some work has been done to account for this scenario [21] [40].

Modeling with BNs brings up many different questions and issues. How does one keep the CPTs small? What about relationships that are not clearly defined? If the network is created purely from subject matter expertise how are disagreements accounted for? How does one optimize network structure? How is time dealt with? The answers to these questions are simply methods of modeling with BNs and are outlined in [21]. Knowing all of these methods is not important to understanding BNs, however, the method of Dynamic Bayesian Networks (DBN) will be briefly addressed. A DBN is a single BN carried through time. At each time step the same network structure exists, but the parameters are updated due to the time step and/or new evidence. Since, BNs are DAGs, DBNs are often used to account for feedback within a specific scenario assuming the feedback occurs over time. It should be pointed out that feedback loops are a significant issue in BNs. What if the situation being modeled required feedback that was not time dependent? Spirtes [59] in his work on Directed Cycle Graphs (DCGs) asserts that certain necessary properties in BNs fail when DCGs are "interpreted by analogy with DAGs as representing functional dependencies with independently distributed noises or "error terms."" Tulupyev and Nikolenko [61] attempt to handle feedback loops within BNs by treating them as a "family of probabilistic distributions rather than a singular distribution." The question of feedback loops within BNs is still very open. Returning to DBNs, Murphy [37] points out in his work that DBNs are typically used to represent Hidden

34

Markov Models (HMMs) or Kalman Filter Models (KFMs). Poropudas is a good reference for further understanding of DBNs as he provides a simple application of DBNs involving aircraft combat [47] and has applied DBNs to simulation metamodeling [48] [49]. An interesting extension to DBNs and very new area are non-stationary DBNs, which are defined by Robinson and Hartemink [53] in their work and extended by Grzegorcyk and Husmeier [18]. Though more work has been done in this area, these two sources offer a good introduction to non-stationary DBNs.

So far, this paper has mainly focused on understanding and manipulating an existing BN, but how does one build the network and determine its parameters? One answer is to simply use subject matter experts to define the relationships between variables or the network structure and to assist in parameterizing the model. Since this method is difficult to validate, research has been and is currently being done to develop sophisticated techniques for learning the BNs from real world or simulated data. Given some data set how can one determine the causal relationship between variables in the data set and generate a valid BN to depict those relationships. Numerous issues arise when trying to generate networks from data. What if the data is sparse or biased? What if the data is just expert opinion? How is this information utilized and validated? How does one determine which variables should be related within the network and can the network be reduced or simplified? Can probability constraints be put in the network? How sensitive are the parameters to changes in the network? All of these questions and many more are concerns when learning a BN. Before these questions are addressed it would be useful to understand the process of learning BNs. Scutari describes the learning process using a package in R called *bnlearn* [55] and Jensen provides a good overview in his book [21]. The first step in learning BNs is to determine structure of the network. There are two basic methods for learning the structure [55]:

Constraint-based algorithms: These algorithms learn the network structure by analyzing the probabilistic relations entailed by the Markov property of Bayesian networks with conditional independence tests and then constructing a graph which satisfies the corresponding d-separation statements. The resulting models are often interpreted as *causal models* even when learned from observational data (Pearl 1988) [43]

Score-based algorithms: These algorithms assign a score to each candidate Bayesian network and try to maximize it with some heuristic search algorithm. Greedy search algorithms are a common choice, but almost any kind of search procedure can be used.

Once the structure has been learned, the parameters or inputs of the CPTs must be determined. The two popular methods for parameterizing are Maximum Likelihood Estimation and Bayesian Estimation [21]:

Maximum Likelihood Estimation: Let $M = (S, \theta)$ be a BN with structure S and parameters θ over the set of variables, U and D a complete data set over all possible cases in the set U. Then one must simply maximize the likelihood of M given $d \epsilon D$:

$$L(M|D) = \prod_{d \epsilon D} P(d|M) \tag{3.5}$$

Bayesian Estimation: This approach starts with a prior distribution on the parameters and uses experience to update distributions.

For more reading on these two methods see [21]. A major problem with these methods and in the area of learning Bayesian Networks from data is the issue of incomplete or sparse data. Liao and Ji categorize missing data into three different areas [31]:

Missing At Random (MAR): The probability of missing data on any variable is not related to its particular value, but could be related to the other variables

Missing Completely at Random (MCAR): The missing value of a variable depends neither on the variable itself nor on the values of other variables in the BN

Not Missing At Random (NMAR): The data found missing depends on the values of the variables

Liao and Ji present an algorithm that uses domain knowledge to learn BNs when large amounts of data are missing. Their work, as well as an earlier literature review by Druzdzel and Gaag [10], also provides a good overview of how missing data has been dealt with in the past [31].

A more efficient method is the Expectation-Maximization (EM) algorithm, which is able to handle missing data. The algorithm can be found in full in [21], but in short:

> The algorithm basically alternates between so-called *expectation step* and a *maximization step*: loosely speaking, in the expectation step, we "complete" the data set by using the current parameter estimates $\hat{\epsilon}$ to calculate expectations for the missing values, and in the maximization step we use the "completed" data set to find a new maximum likelihood estimate $\hat{\epsilon}'$ for the parameters. This estimate is then used to complete the data set in the next iteration of the algorithm. The algorithm continues either for a predetermined number of iterations or until the algorithm has converged.

Having a learned or created a BN it is important to make the network more efficient and accurate by removing unnecessary nodes or adding missing nodes, combining certain events, adding or removing arcs, etc. Chang and Fung [5] discuss two of these modifications to BNs as refining or coarsening the network. Refinement is the "introduction of new distinctions to a state space [of the BN]" and coarsening refers to the "removal of distinctions" within a state space [5]. States that can be altered are specific nodes and their CPTs. Their work develops techniques for "emphasizing" relevant states within a network and giving less emphasis to or absorbing lower weighted states. Peng and Ding's research developed a derivative of the Iterative Proportional Fitting Procedure (IPFP) that modifies an existing BN subject to certain probability constraints while still retaining its structure and remaining as close as possible to the original BN based upon the *Kullback-Leibler distance* [44]. In Flores et al.'s [15] work, they look at the reuse of join trees in changing BNs. Their work focuses on structural changes, such as adding or removing nodes, as opposed to the probability constraints considered in Peng and Ding [44]. These are just a few examples of the current work being done to modify BNs.

Once the BN has been created, parameterized, modified and the propagation technique decided upon the next step is to perform sensitivity analysis on the network. Sensitivity analysis is concerned with how the network is effected when a specific query or hypothesis is made. Koski and Nobe [28] define queries as:

Probability Updating: If evidence, e, is given on some variables, find the posterior probability potentials for the rest of the variables in the network

Most Probable Configuration: If evidence, e, is given on the variables in a set U, find the most probable values of the rest of the variables.

Maximum Aposterior (MAP) Hypothesis: If evidence, e is given on some variables in a set U, find a hypothesis h over a subset of variables which maximizes the probability $p(h|e)$

Jensen and Nielsen [21] refer to hypothesis as "events that are not directly observable (or observable only at an unacceptable cost)." [21] Sensitivity analysis seeks to answer the following questions outlined in [28] as they relate to different queries or hypothesis.

1. How does one bound the changes made to parameters within a BN?

2. When updates are made to a BN, how does one bound the distance between the original network and updated network?

3. How relevant is a specific parameter to some query constraint and what is the minimum amount of change that a parameter needs to satisfy the constraint?

4. How sensitive is a query to some parameter change.

Before answering these questions some method must be developed to uniformly change parameters and some technique for determining distance between distributions. Parameters in CPTs can be related linearly using proportionally scaling [28] [21] and a popular distance or divergence measure for probability distributions is the Chan-Darwiche distance measure [28].

Definition 3.1.4 *Let p and q be two probability functions over a finite state space X. That is, $p : X \to [0,1]$ and $q : X \to [0,1]$, $\Sigma_{x \epsilon X} p(x) = 1$ and $\Sigma_{x \epsilon X} q(x) = 1$. The Chain-Darwiche distance is defined as*

$$D_{CD}(p,q) = logmax_{x \epsilon X} \frac{q(x)}{p(x)} - logmin_{x \epsilon X} \frac{q(x)}{p(x)} \tag{3.6}$$

where, by definition, $\frac{0}{0} = 1$ and $\frac{+\inf}{+\inf} = 1$.

Using these tools [28] is able to answer these sensitivity analysis questions. For more reading on sensitivity analysis see [28] [21] [8]. Also, NETICA offers some sensitivity analysis, specifically, theory in determining mutual information between nodes.

The goal of this paper was to provide a basic understanding of Bayesian Networks, an overview of the current research areas within Bayesian Networks and useful references. For further reading on Bayesian Networks in general Chen and Pollino seek to develop a general framework for Bayesian Network modeling in their work [6]. Boutilier et al. [2] discuss independence relations in BNs. Sierra et al. [57] and Hulten et al. [20] discuss BN learning using histogram distances for classification purposes and from dependency networks respectively. Pearl [42] [43] and Neapolitan [39] are good sources on the early developments of BNs and for more current reading regarding general BN techniques [28], [26] and [8] are useful books alongside Jensen and Nielsen's work [21]. Finally, for information concerning BN learning algorithms Murphy provides an exhaustive list of BN learning tools [34].

IV. Fitting Dynamic Bayesian Networks to Simulated Data with Bootstrapping

4.1 Introduction

The use of Modeling and Simulation (M&S) is becoming more and more widespread. The growth in computing power means M&S applications can represent increasingly complex systems at increasing levels of fidelity. These higher fidelity models have further enhanced the insight provided to decision makers relying on those models. Unfortunately, these larger more complex models still require large amounts of computational effort. When decision time constraints prohibit the running of these models to answer specific questions, metamodels can be exploited to quickly obtain answers aligned with answers derived directly from the complex models.

Simulation metamodels provide useful analytical solutions and insight into the larger models, but require much less computing power and respond in a much quicker time. Metamodel development is predicated on the ability to run the full model a sufficient number of times to collect the results upon which the metamodel is built. Typically the full model is run using input parameters set to capture the full range of inputs. These efforts will quite often yield very large experimental designs, thus analytical planning should allow the collection of this data before periods of time-critical decision-making. Then in time-critical moments, when analytical solutions are needed quickly, these metamodels can provide a necessary alternative to the time-consuming large-scale simulations.

There are two major limitations to metamodels. One, they are typically simple input-output models implying that they do not provide probabilistic insight into the outputs based upon single inputs. Secondly, as [49] point out, current metamodels do not capture the time aspect present in numerous simulations. Porpudas and Virtanen propose the Dynamic Bayesian Network (DBN) as a useful metamodel for simulations and their work is the leading research done in this area [47] - [49] [51]. Poropudas has used a DBN as a metamodel of queuing systems and air-to-air, engagement-level models. Pousi et al. [51] introduce a lower bound for the number of simulations (or replicates) needed to train the DBN per input experimental design setting. Their approach [51] first formulates a confidence interval for a probability estimate, $\hat{\tau} = P(A = a | B = b)$, taken from the DBN [51]:

$$\hat{\tau} \pm z_{\alpha/2}\sqrt{Var(\hat{\tau})} \tag{4.1}$$

where $Var(\hat{\tau}) = \hat{\tau}(1 - \hat{\tau})/\mathcal{N}_b$ and $\mathcal{N}_b$ is the number of simulation runs such that $B = b$. Next, let $r = z_{\alpha/2}\sqrt{Var(\hat{\tau})}$, N be the number of input variables, R the number of possible values pertaining to each input variable and f the probability of the least likely combination of inputs or instances within the DBN. Now using f and the half-width for the confidence interval of some probability estimate, τ, in the DBN, a lower bound for the necessary number of simulation runs for a given design setting is defined as [51]

$$\mathcal{N} \geq z^2_{1-\alpha/2}/(4 \cdot R^N \cdot f \cdot r^2). \tag{4.2}$$

Using Equation 4.2 and rounding up implies using 10,000 simulations at each experimental setting to train the DBN, for $f = 0.05$, $r = 0.05$, $N = 1$ and $R = 1$. Most analysts cannot expect to receive 10,000 model replicates for each design point within an experimental design spanning the full ranges of model input parameter values. To effectively train and employ a DBN, the number of required replicates must be reduced. This paper introduces bootstrapping techniques to address this replicate problem. The paper is organized as follows. Section 2 outlines the bootstrapping technique utilized. Section 3 discuses multiple goodness of fit tests, examined to validate the bootstrap results to include the Kullback-Leibler divergence as a goodness of fit test for validation. Section 4 presents a methodological approach used to test the bootstrapping approach. Section 5 provides the results and section 6 the concluding remarks.

4.2 Bootstrapping

Bootstrapping is a simulation resampling technique often used to estimate parameters of a distribution when only a small sample from the distribution is available. Given a random sample from the underlying distribution being studied, resampling holds that one can obtain another (or larger) random sample by randomly sampling from the current sample [4]. Bootstrapping was first introduced in [11] and is currently an accepted and widely used technique. Though there are various specific approaches to bootstrapping, this paper uses the basic algorithm used by [4]. Suppose you have the statistic θ estimated from a random sample set of observations $X = \{X_1, X_2, ..., X_n\}$. To create a bootstrapped data set, $X^* = \{X_1^*, X_2^*, ..., X_n^*\}$, sample from X with replacement n times using $P(X_i^* = X_i) = 1/n \; \forall \; i \; \epsilon \; \{1, 2, ..., n\}$. The bootstrap statistic, θ^*, calculated from X^*, is now an estimator for θ. As more bootstrap samples are generated the distribution moments of θ can be estimated from sample moments of θ^* [4]. The benefit of bootstrapping is the use of a sample set, X, to yield improved precision in the estimation of θ.

The application of bootstrapping presented in this paper is quite novel in two respects. First, rather than bootstrapping from a set of values to estimate some statistic of interest, the proposed application bootstraps from a set of simulation runs to estimate the time indexed set of probability distribution functions in the DBN. The comparison challenge then becomes a comparison among distribution functions. The second novel aspect is the use of bootstrapping as a way to reduce the sample size (i.e., the actual number of simulation experiments) of results used to create the bootstrap sample used to train the DBN.

For more detailed reading on bootstrapping see [11] [13] [12] [63]. [4] provides a good example of how bootstrapping is used in the context of military modeling.

4.3 Data Comparison Techniques

There are multiple goodness of fit techniques that can be used to test the equivalence of two distributions. Typical goodness of fit tests include the Chi-Square(CS), Anderson-Darling (AD) and Kolmogorov-Smirnov (KS) tests. These three tests are widely used and considered in this work. These tests determine if the observed data differ from an assumed underlying distribution. The AD and KS tests offer 2-sample test versions which determine if the underlying distributions of a pair of observed variables differ. Porpudas and Virtanen initially use the CS test [49], but then switch to the 2-sample AD test in later papers [51]. Thus, we do not test the CS test in this research.

The research goal is to assess whether simulated data generated via bootstrap sampling produces a sufficiently accurate DBN. The assessment of any DBN involves comparing the Cumulative Distribution Functions (CDF) of the bootstrap sample trained DBN to the CDFs of the DBN trained using the "valid" data set, that set based on the non-bootstrapped data. This approach implies that 2-sample tests are appropriate. Therefore only the 2-sample tests are discussed. This section presents the 2-sample KS test, 2-sample AD test and proposes a 2-sample goodness of fit test based upon the Kullback-Leibler (KL) divergence. The discussion justifies use of the KS-test in section 4.

4.3.1   2-Sample Anderson-Darling Goodness of Fit Test.

The 2-Sample AD goodness of fit test is outlined in [54] with references to its origin
in [7] and further studies of the test in [46]. Given two empirical CDFs, $P_n(x)$ and
$Q_m(x)$ based on random samples $X = \{X_1, X_2, ..., X_n\}$ and $X^* = \{X_1^*, X_2^*, ...X_m^*\}$,
respectively, the 2-Sample AD test statistic is formulated as follows:

$$A_{nm}^2 = \frac{mn}{N} \int_{-\infty}^{\infty} \frac{\{P_n(x) - Q_m(x)\}^2}{H_N(x)\{1 - H_N(x)\}} \tag{4.3}$$

where $H_N(x) = \frac{\{nP_n(x) + mQ_m(x)\}}{N}$ and $N = m + n$. The null hypothesis for the AD
test is that $P_n(x) = Q_m(x)$ and a failure to reject the null hypothesis would imply
that there is not enough evidence to assume that the data sets come from different
distributions. The AD test was designed to be "sensitive to discrepancies at the tails
of the distribution rather than near the median" [1]. This research is, currently, not
as concerned with the tails of the distributions which translate to the extreme cases or
least likely outputs of the simulation. Also, it is common practice to use the KS test
over the AD test when dealing with larger data sets. For these reasons the comparison
results for the AD test are not presented in this paper, though future research should
utilize the AD test to consider the extreme cases.

4.3.2   2-Sample Kolmogorov-Smirnov Goodness of Fit Test.

The second test is the more common 2-Sample KS test. [16] argue for using the
probability distributions instead of the means as a comparison technique for different
systems. As Friedman and Friedman note, "just because two systems [queuing sys-
tems] have the same average waiting time does not mean that they are equivalent. In
fact, the entire output distributions may be significantly different with the only sim-
ilarity between the two systems being that mean value" [16]. The 2-Sample KS test

is introduced as a suitable method for comparing distributions of different systems and they argue that the robustness of the KS test determines variations between the systems in "location, dispersion, or skewness" [16]. Given two empirical CDFs, $P_n(x)$ and $Q_m(x)$, The KS test statistic is

$$D_{n,m} = \sup_x |P_n(x) - Q_m(x)|. \tag{4.4}$$

The 2-Sample KS test determines if the underlying distributions from two different data sets are equivalent. The null hypothesis is that the two samples have the same underlying distribution. If the KS statistic is less than the critical value the test will fail to reject the null hypothesis indicating that there is not enough evidence to assume that the two data sets come from different distributions. The KS test focuses on the largest deviation between the CDFs of the two samples being compared. The KS test is commonly used for large data sets and is the method of comparison presented in Section 5.5.

4.3.3 Kullback-Leibler Divergence Goodness of Fit Test.

[58] first introduced the KL divergence as a goodness of fit method and it is further studied by [30]. Song points to the simplicity of his KL method, the fact that it is non-parametric and it does not require smoothness conditions [58]. This paper introduces a different version of the KL test as a means for comparing DBNs.

Given two data sets $X = \{X_1, X_2, ..., X_n\}$ and $X^* = \{X_1^*, X_2^*, ..., X_m^*\}$ their respective empirical CDFs can be calculated as $P_n(x)$ and $Q_m(x)$. Assuming that $P_n(x)$ and $Q_m(x)$ are significantly close, one can compare the divergence between $P_n(x)$ and $Q_m(x)$. There are many divergences available, but one of the most commonly used

46

divergences is the Kullback-Leibler (KL), defined as

$$D_{KL}(P||Q) = \int_{-\infty}^{+\infty} P(x) \log \frac{P(x)}{Q(x)} dx. \tag{4.5}$$

The issue with using any divergence to compare empirical distributions is that there is no point of reference or threshold with which to determine if the distributions are significantly close. The farther the divergence is from zero, the farther apart the distributions are, but how close to zero does the divergence have to be for the distributions to be significantly close? We address this problem using Monte Carlo Simulation to generate empirically the quantities needed for a goodness of fit test specific to the current research focus.

First, 10,000 data points were used to generate an empirical CDF, $G(x)$, and its probability distribution function (pdf), $g(x)$. These data points were generated from both a normal distribution and an exponential distribution to account for different shapes in probability distribution functions. Next, 10,000 new data points are randomly generated from $g(x)$ and a new CDF is created $G^*(x)$. The KL divergence is then used to compare $G(x)$ and $G^*(x)$. This procedure is repeated 100,000 times producing 100,000 divergence values. Then the 95th percentile of the 100,000 KL divergences is used as the threshold for a significance level of $\alpha = 0.05$. The results indicated that a KL divergence value of approximately 0.0008 is the threshold for a significance level of $\alpha = 0.05$. Other values for α can be determined by simply changing the percentile of interest, as indicated in Table 1.

Unfortunately, the KL method presented in this paper requires much more development and testing before it can be used. The goal is to create a KL goodness of fit test that is not greatly affected by sample size, discretization and distribution shape. This present method, however, has only been developed for exponential and normal distributions and no analysis has been done to determine sensitivity to sample size

Table 1. KL Thresholds

Normal		Exponential	
Alpha	Threshold	Alpha	Threshold
0.15	0.000514578	0.15	0.000600334
0.1	0.000589171	0.1	0.000668612
0.05	0.000745798	0.05	0.000776999
0.01	0.00243698	0.01	0.001006275

and discretization. It is simply presented here as a possible future goodness of fit test.

4.4   Analytical Methodology

Robust empirical results require large sample sizes to best reflect corresponding theoretical results. Obtaining such large sample sizes favor quick running models. While our focus is meta-models of large scale models, for this methodological development we prefer a simplified model with known theoretical properties. A well-known and analytically favored model is a queueing model. Such models can be efficiently executed and have known theoretical properties. For the current setting, the concern is less with the theoretical results but more with the empirical results and the potential impact of the proposed bootstrapping methodology.

An $M/M/1$ queuing model is simulated using MATLAB$^{\copyright}$ to test the bootstrapping method. Recall an $M/M/1$ model involves a single server system with customers arriving via a Poisson process (Markovian) and experience exponential service times (Markovian). The current model uses a mean service rate of $\mu = 2.5$ and mean inter-arrival rate $\lambda = 1.5$. The simulation was run 10,000 times returning the number of customers in the system, L_t, at 11 specific time steps, $t \in T$, where $T = 0, 1, 2, ..., 10$. To approximate steady-state, the queue was initialized with one customer in service having a service time of 2.5 and one customer in queue. The data was then used to fit a DBN such as shown in Figure 15 using the suggested sample size of 10,000 simulation runs as the baseline. Thus, a set of 10,000 runs of the $M/M/1$ model represents the "ground truth" for the current study. A DBN model based on these 10,000 runs is what a bootstrapping methodology should replicate, but based on significantly fewer actual model runs. The empirical study focuses on using a subset of the 10,000 runs to create the bootstrapped 10,000 run data set which is then used to create the bootstrap DBN. The "ground truth" DBN is then compared to the bootstrap DBN. To compare DBNs, the pdf for the response of interest, L_t, is extracted at each of 11 ($t = 0, 1, ..., 10$) time steps and the corresponding CDFs are created. These CDFs, one each from the "ground truth" and bootstrap DBN, are then statistically compared. This comparison process is replicated and examined for various bootstrap sizes.

At this point, it is necessary to establish some consistent notation. Let $y_{j,t}$ be defined as the number of customers in the system at time step $t = 0, ..., 10$ in simulation replication $j = 1, ..., 10,000$. The experiment involves 100 macro-replications where each macro-replication generates a 10,000 replication simulation result. The data for each macro-replication is expressed as

$$Y^i = \{y_{j,t} : j = 1, ..., 10,000;\ t = 0, ..., 10\},\ \text{for i} = 1,...,100\ \text{macro-replications}$$

$$(4.6)$$

Each Y^i is used to generate a DBN denoted as D_0^i to represent "ground truth," for macro-replication i. Subsets of each Y^i are extracted to represent the bootstrap samples. For a bootstrap sub-sample of size b, we get

$$Y_b^i = \{y_{j,t} : j = 1, ..., b;\ t = 0, ..., 10\},\ \text{for i} = 1,...,100\ \text{macro-replications} \quad (4.7)$$

as the bootstrap sample of size b for macro-replication i. This will lead, upon expansion via bootstrapping, to DBN, D_b^i which will be compared to D_0^i for each i and every b subset considered.

This D_0^i to D_b^i comparison is accomplished multiple times (100 in this experiment). Thus, the experiment generates 100 instances of D_b^i, denoted as $D_{b,k}^i$, $k = 1, ..., 100$, for each macro-replication i and each considered bootstrap size b.

Define $g(Y_b^i)$ as the function that returns a bootstrap instance from the bootstrap sample Y_b^i. Then create

$$Y_{b,k}^i = Y_b^i \cup \{\cup_{l=1}^{m-b} g(Y_b^i)\}, \text{ s.t. } m \geq 10,000 \text{ and } k = 1, ..., 100 \qquad (4.8)$$

as the full data set from the bootstrap sample data set used to train $D_{b,k}^i$.

Each DBN has pdfs at each time step, $t = 0, ..., 10$. These pdfs are used to generate the CDFs that are statistically compared. From D_0^i extract the pdf

$$f_t^i(x) = pr(x = X : x \, \epsilon \, X_t^i), \; t = 0, ...10 \qquad (4.9)$$

where X_t^i is the discrete set of possible values of the number of customers in the system at time step t for macro-replicaiton i. Similarly, from $D_{b,k}^i$ extract the pdf

$$f_{t,b,k}^i(x) = pr(x = X : x \, \epsilon \, X_t^i), \; t = 0, ...10 \qquad (4.10)$$

where X_t^i is the same discrete set generated for the full data set Y^i from which the bootstrap sample Y_b^i is extracted. We use $\{750, 1500, 2250, 3000\}$ as the set of bootstrap sample sizes from which b is defined.

From each pdf, corresponding CDFs are generated, denoted as $F_t^i(x)$ and $F_{t,b,k}^i(x)$ respectively. It is these CDFs that are compared using the techniques outlined in section 4.3.

4.5 Results

As noted in Section 4.3, only the results of the KS test are presented. These results are summarized in Figures 16 - 18.

The KS test is applied to CDFs $F_t^i(x)$ and $F_{t,b,k}^i(x)$ for all values of t, b, k and i returning a 1 if the test accepts the null hypothesis and 0 otherwise using $\alpha = 0.01$. Let $I_{0,1}(i, t, b, k, x)$ be an indicator function that returns 1 if the KS test accepts the null and 0 otherwise. For simulated data set Y^i, denote the KS acceptance rate for time step t and bootstrap sample size b as $\bar{\Theta}_{t,i,b}$ and the average KS acceptance rate over all macro-replications i as $\bar{\Theta}_{t,\cdot,b}$. These values are defined in equations 4.11 - 4.14.

$$\Theta_{t,i,b} = \Sigma_{k=1}^{100} I_{0,1}(i, t, b, k, x) \tag{4.11}$$

$$\bar{\Theta}_{t,i,b} = \Theta_{t,i,b}/100. \tag{4.12}$$

$$\Theta_{t,\cdot,b} = \Sigma_{i=1}^{100} \bar{\Theta}_{t,i,b} \tag{4.13}$$

$$\bar{\Theta}_{t,\cdot,b} = \Theta_{t,\cdot,b}/100. \tag{4.14}$$

The proportion of time indexed pdfs/CDFs that pass the KS test for macro-replication i, bootstrap sample size b and bootstrapped data replication k is defined in equations 4.15 and 4.16.

$$\Theta_{\cdot,i,b} = \Sigma_{t=0}^{10} \Theta_{t,i,b} \tag{4.15}$$

$$\bar{\Theta}_{\cdot,i,b} = \Theta_{\cdot,i,b}/11. \tag{4.16}$$

51

Figures 16 and 17 are the plots of $\bar{\Theta}_{t,\cdot,b}$ and $\bar{\Theta}_{\cdot,i,b}$, respectively, for each bootstrap sample size b. From Figure 16, dropping to a bootstrap sample size of $b = 1,500$ means the CDFs (pdfs) match over 95% of the time at each of the time steps examined, except for t_1 and t_2, indicating that some transient behavior is still present in the model. This transient behavior is also observed in Figure 18. Figure 17 plots the KS test acceptance rate for each "ground truth" DBN, D_0^i. Again, we see that a bootstrap sample size of $b = 1500$ will, on average, ensure an acceptable DBN 95% of the time and almost 100% of the time for $b = 3000$. Figure 18 plots $\bar{\Theta}_{t,i,b}$ versus bootstrap sample size for each time step t with $\alpha = 0.01$.

Based on the KS test results, bootstrap sample sizes of 2,250 or possibly 1,500 will produce data sets statistically close to a simulated data set of 10,000 with a small chance of the KS test rejecting the null hypothesis at one or two time steps t. 1,500 simulation runs is still a large number of runs, but significantly better than 10,000 runs.

Next, the sensitivity to the choice of α is explored. The results in Figures 16 - 18 were generated using an $\alpha = 0.01$. For each bootstrap sample size, b, the number of KS acceptances are averaged over all 100×100 macro and bootstrap replications $(i \times k)$ and all 11 time steps for $\alpha \in \{0.01, 0.03, 0.05\}$.

$$\Theta_{\cdot,\cdot,b} = \Sigma_{t=0}^{10} \bar{\Theta}_{t,\cdot,b} \tag{4.17}$$

$$\bar{\Theta}_{\cdot,\cdot,b} = \Theta_{\cdot,\cdot,b}/11 \tag{4.18}$$

The KS averages are plotted against α in Figure 19. Figure 19 indicates that for an α equal to 0.01 or even 0.03 the researcher can confidently use a bootstrap sample size of 2,250 with a small chance of only one variable failing the KS test. In fact, one could drop to 1,500 as a bootstrap sample size and still have acceptable confidence in the bootstrapped DBN.

As a final litmus test, Figure 20 is a DBN fit to a random bootstrapped data set generated from the first 1,500 runs of the data used to create Figure 15. The α is set to 0.01. The KS test fails to reject the null hypothesis for all time steps t implying that there is not enough evidence to assume the underlying distributions for the simulated data are different from the bootstrapped data. In turn, this implies that the bootstrapped DBN in Figure 20 is a suitable estimate for the ground truth DBN in Figure 15. Note that this is one iteration of bootstrap sampling. If the sample data were bootstrapped again and compared, the KS test has a small chance of failing at one or two of the time steps t.

4.6 Conclusions

DBNs can be useful meta-models, but require many data points to train. Bootstrapping is an accepted method for estimating the parameters of a distribuiton from a small data sample. This research is a first look at utilizing bootstrapping to create useful DBN metamodels based on fewer simulation runs. DBNs based on larger samples are trained and compared to DBNs trained on bootstrapped data. CDFs derived from the DBNs are compared. Three goodness of fit tests are discussed. The KL and AD tests are introduced but were found not particularly useful; a KL test is a proposed method of comparison in the bootstrapping application, but needs further development before being useful and the AD test is too sensitive to differences in the tails. The KS test is the test used and indicates that bootstrap sample sizes of 1,500 - 2,250 can produce significantly accurate DBNs, while reducing to a bootstrap sample size of 750 or lower may still be practical, when considering a DBN built from 10,000 simulation runs as "ground-truth".

A major limitation to a simple bootstrapping technique used in this work is its inability to account for the rare events in simulation; those events in the tails of the outcome distribution. If the smaller sample data fails to include the extreme cases, such as might be realized in a larger sample, the DBN metamodel cannot capture them. For future research more sophisticated rare-event simulation techniques might be used to capture the extremities of the outcome distribution. When these extremities are captured, it might be useful to use the AD test giving more weight to the tails when comparing distributions.

Our results indicate that bootstrapping is a useful technique and can significantly reduce the number of actual simulation runs necessary to train a DBN as a simulation meta-model.

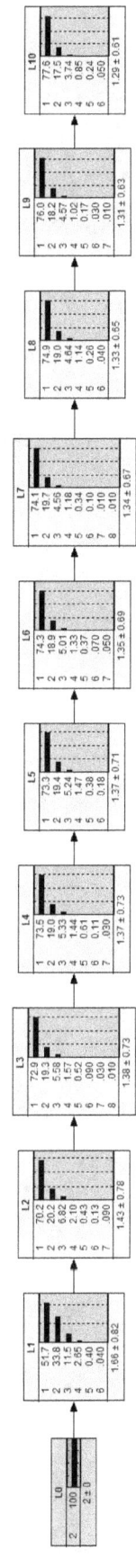

Figure 15. "Ground Truth" DBN, D_0, trained on 10,000 simulation runs. The figure depicts the pdfs at each of the time steps used in the comparison. This DBN represents the true DBN for one macro-replication of the experiment.

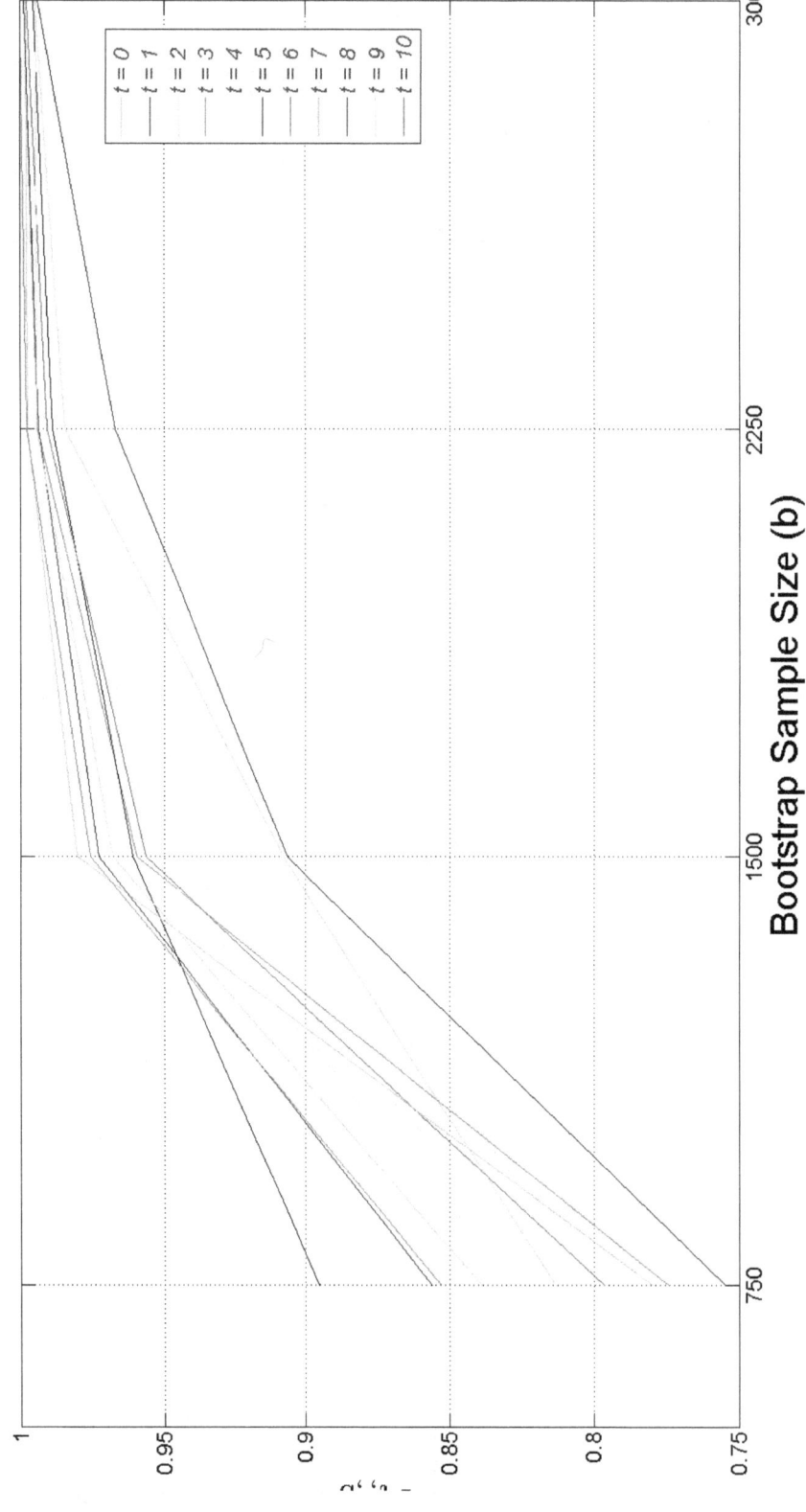

Figure 16. Average KS Test Acceptance Rate Across Bootstrap Sample Size b for Each Time Step t and $\alpha = 0.01$

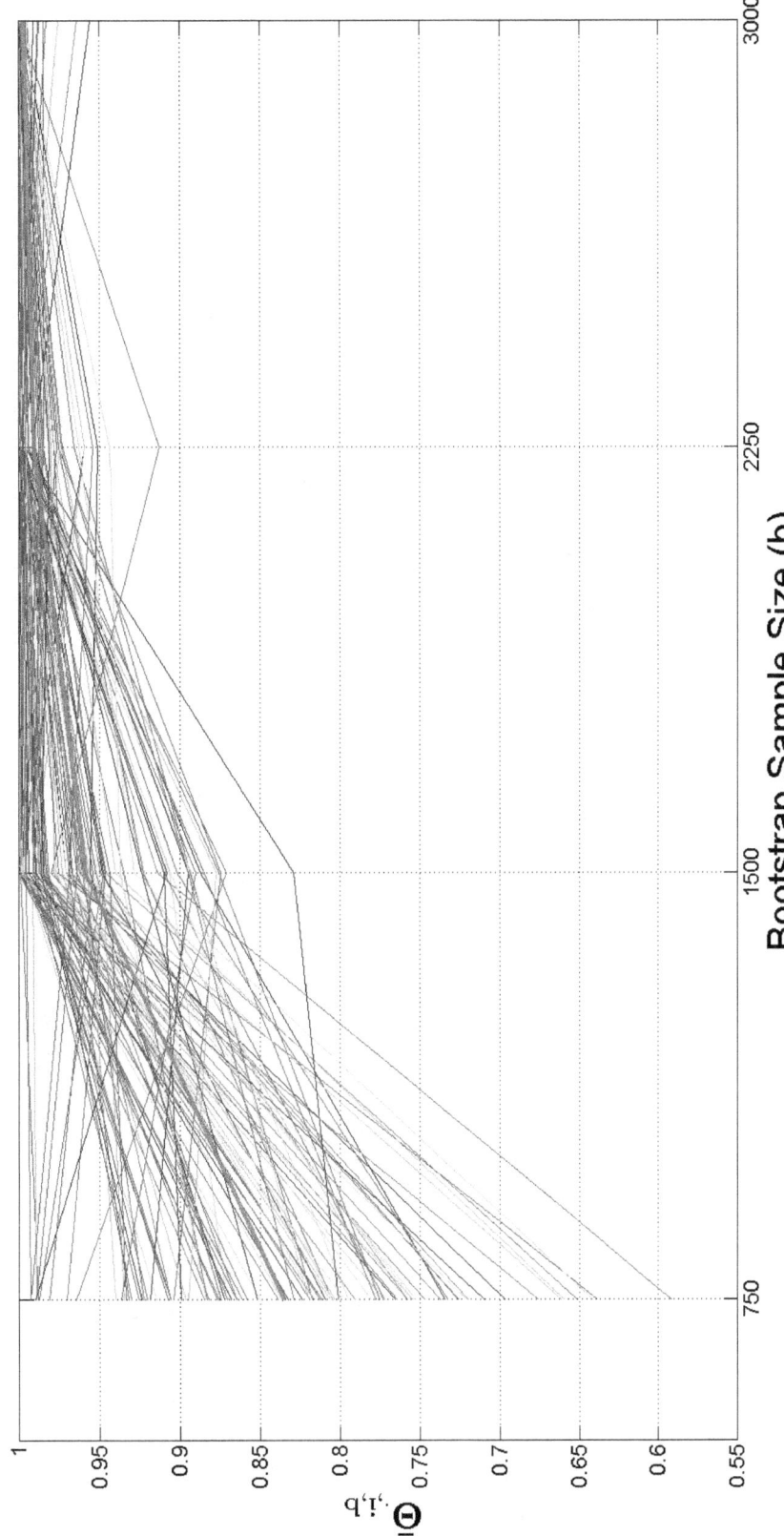

Figure 17. KS Test Acceptance Rate Across Bootstrap Sample Size b for Each Macro-Replication i at $\alpha = 0.01$

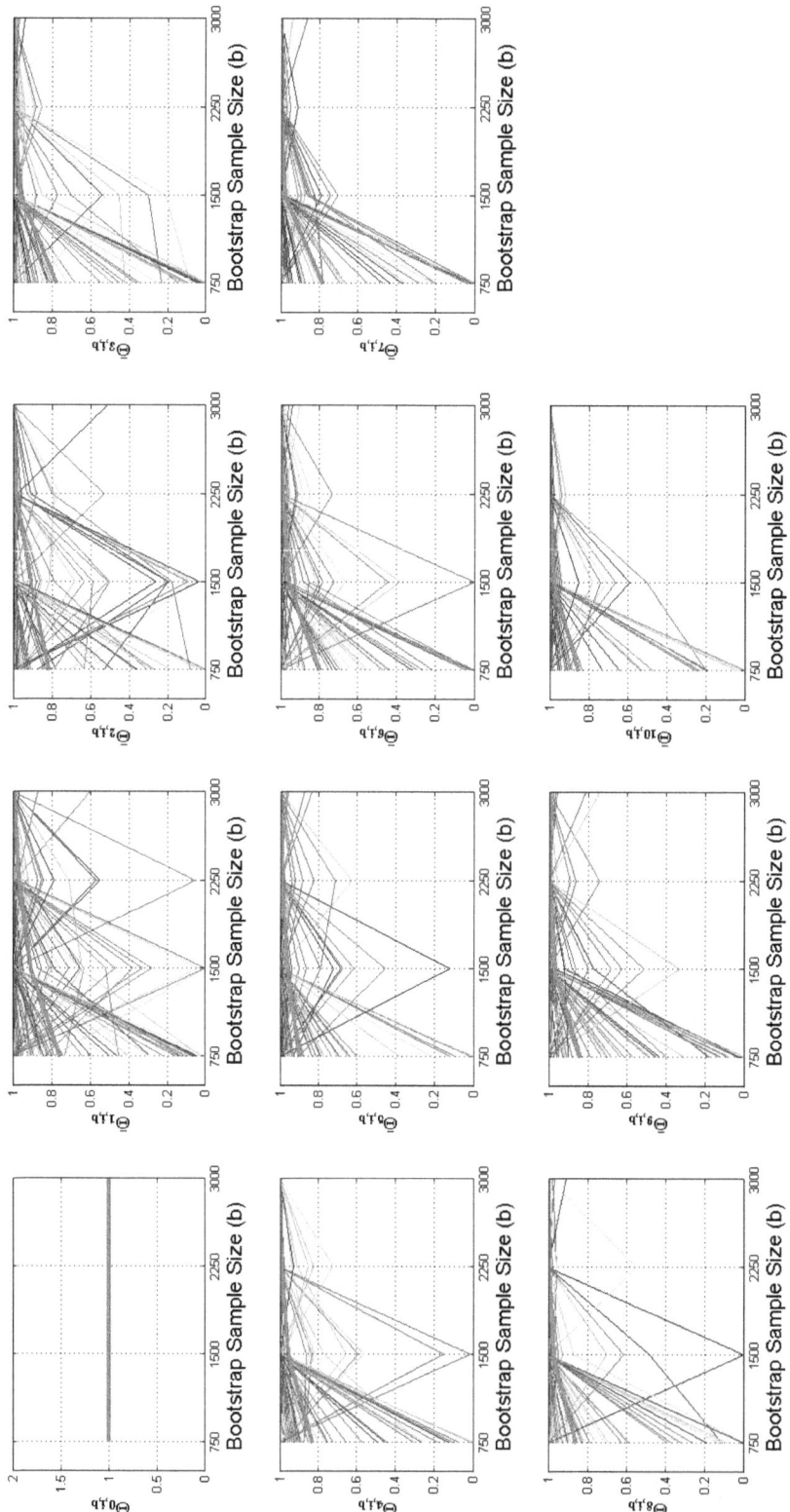

Figure 18. KS Test Acceptance Rate Across Bootstrap Sample Size b for Each Time Step $t \in T$ at $\alpha = 0.01$

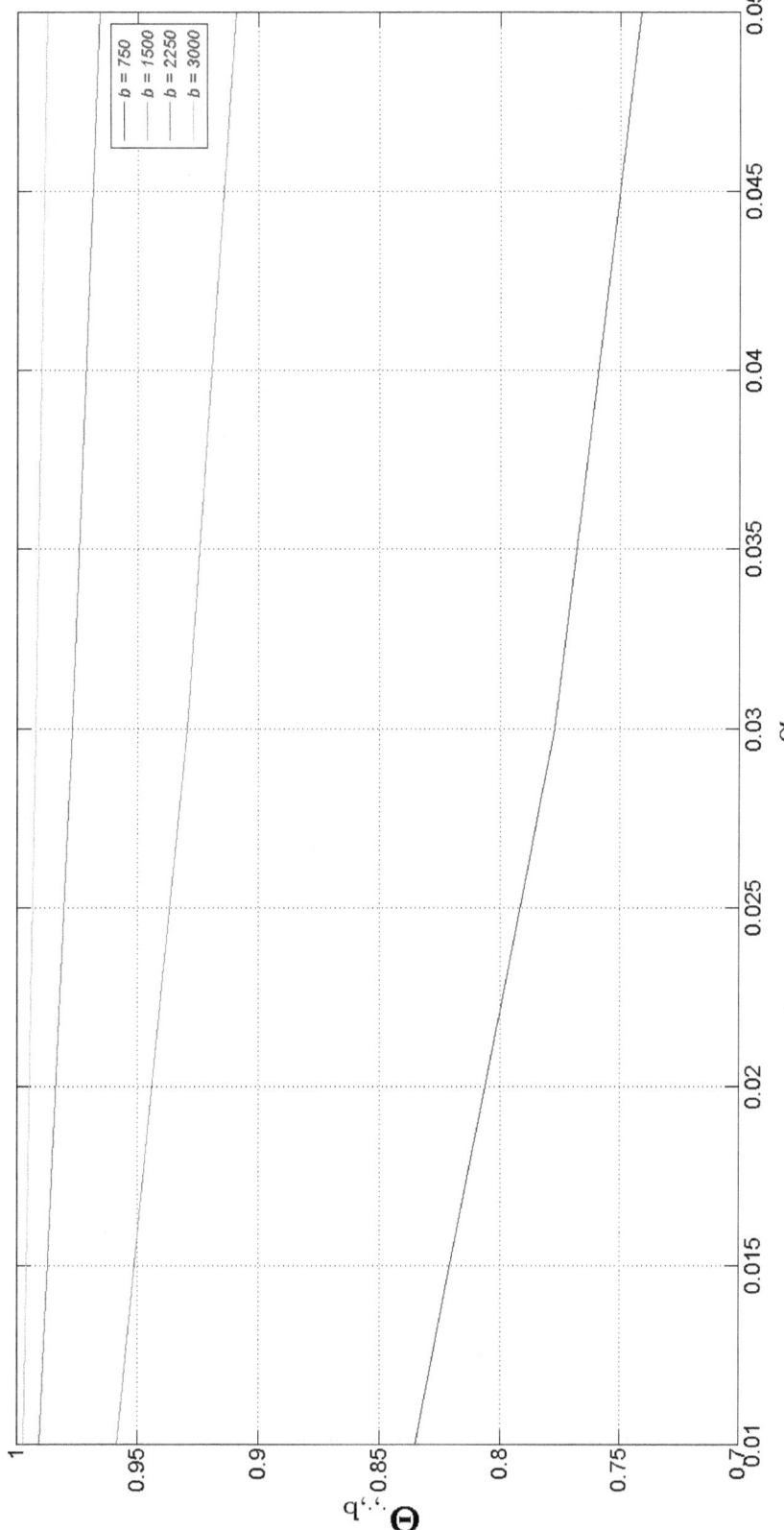

Figure 19. Average KS Acceptance Rate for Various Bootstrap Sizes Across $\alpha \in \{0.01, 0.03, 0.05\}$

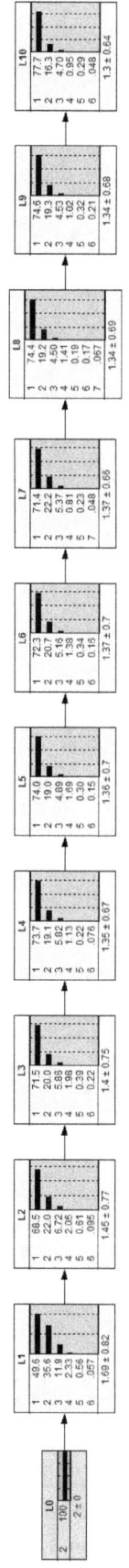

Figure 20. DBN Trained from Bootstrapped Data with Sample Size $b = 1,500$. We can visually compare to D_0^i in Figure 15

V. Reducing the Number of Runs Necessary To Fit a Dynamic Bayesian Network to Simulated Data Using Response Surface Methodologies

5.1 Introduction

Modeling and Simulation (M&S) is a useful analytical tool when an exact solution is too complicated to calculate directly. Unfortunately, many simulations are complex and time-consuming to run "on-demand." Meta-models are used to estimate the outputs of the simulation for some given set of inputs. While there are many metamodels available Poropudas and Virtanen argue for the use of Dynamic Bayesian Networks (DBN) as suitable metamodels [49] [48], in part because they provide a probabilistic element to the metamodel prediction. Unfortunately, the DBN learning process requires a large number of simulation runs to train the networks. The methods introduced in [24] demonstrate that the number of required simulation runs could be significantly reduced through the use of bootstrapping. Prior work using a DBN as a metamodel focused on a single design point or a single dimension of inputs. Practice requires a DBN metamodel represent a full region of interest. This research extends past work by considering experimental designs to cover the region of interest and improved interpolation methods facilitating the use of DBNs for analytic practice.

The paper is organized as follows. Section 2 outlines the experimental designs considered in the analysis. Section 3 discusses the interpolation methods used to estimate design space points from the DBN. Section 4 presents the methodological approach used to test the coverage for each experimental design considered, section 5 provides the results and section 6 the concluding remarks.

5.2   Design Spaces

Design of Experiments (DOE) is an important field of study in a wide variety of fields. Recent interest in the design of computer experiments further attest to the broad applicability of DOE [27] [23]. As applied to M&S, the experimental design goal is to efficiently span the input parameter space to effectively model the output response surface, a surface that may be highly nonlinear. The same motivations for M&S experimental design response surface modeling apply to the current focus on DBN modeling of the response space.

Full examination of the wide variety of experimental designs is beyond the scope of this work. Interested readers are referred to [38] or [67]. The focus of this work is on three of the more common M&S designs: a Full Factorial Design, Central Composite Design (CCD) and the Space Filling Design (specifically the Maximum-Entropy based design).

5.2.1   Full Factorial Design.

Factorial designs are a popular technique for fitting at least an intial response surface. Factorial designs permit estimation of first-order factors and their interaction. These designs are the "very special case that each of the factors has only two levels" [38], thus a factorial design in k factors has 2^k design points in the design. These design points involve every possible combination of upper (max_i) and lower values (min_i) of the factors. Once the upper and lower level values have been determined for each factor, all factor settings, ξ_i, are translated or encoded to lie between 1 and -1 respectively using Equation 5.1. Analysis is generally conducted in this coded space.

$$X_i = \frac{\xi_i - [max_i + min_i]/2}{[max_i - min_i]/2} \tag{5.1}$$

For an experiment considering two factors, A and B, a coded full factorial design is found in Table 2 while Table 3 provides a 2^3 design

Table 2. Full Factorial Design for Two Factors, 2^2

A	B
1	1
-1	1
1	-1
-1	-1

Table 3. Full Factorial Design for Three Factors, 2^3

A	B	C
1	1	1
-1	1	1
1	-1	1
-1	-1	1
1	1	-1
-1	1	-1
1	-1	-1
-1	-1	-1

Figures 21 and 22 display Tables 2 and 3 graphically, respectively. Linear Regression is used to estimate the response surface based on the system response corresponding to each design point.

Major limitations of the factorial design include its use of just two levels limiting the response surface model to linear. To test for nonlinearity experimental runs may be done at the center of the design space or when the inputs have coded values of 0. If non-linearity is determined, then a factorial design may not be the most appropriate method, but can be augmented into a more appropriate design. Also, the number of experimental runs necessary for a full factorial design grows exponentially as more factors are introduced which may be infeasible depending on the cost or duration of each run and the overall experimental budget.

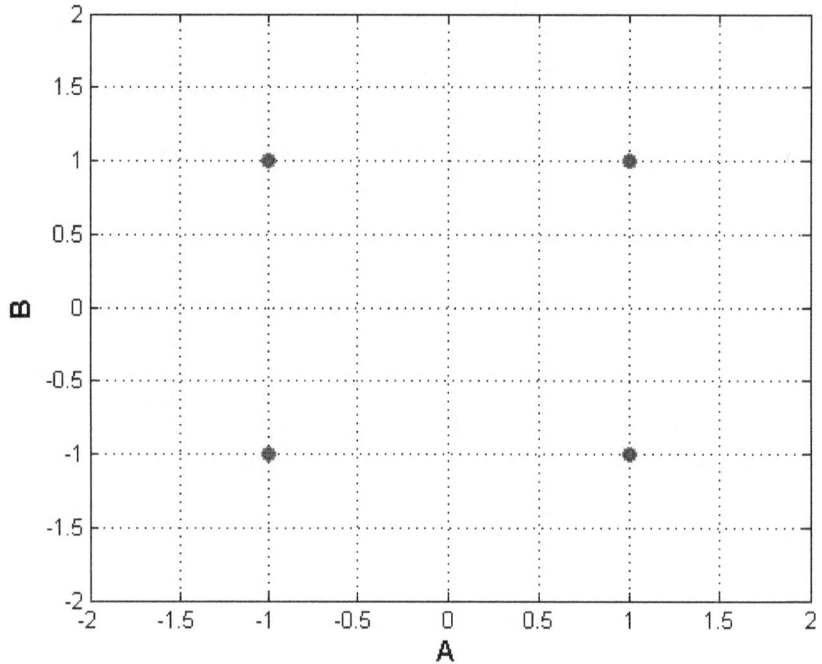

Figure 21. Graphic of a 2^2 design in coded space.

5.2.2 Central Composite Design.

The CCD is recognized as one of the most widely used second-order designs [38]. All CCDs must satisfy two conditions [38]):

1. Each design variable must have at least three levels, andd

2. The design space must have at least $1 + 2k + k(k-1)/2$ design points for k factors.

The coded inputs for a standard CCD with two factors are shown in Table 4 and their plot in Figure 23. Notice that the CCD is an extension of the Full Factorial design, but includes center point runs and axial runs. Axial runs are the runs that step just outside the upper and lower levels of the design space on each input parameter axis and provide the means to estimate any quadratic effects in the response. The CCD is a popular result of augmenting a factorial design to estimate nonlinear effects.

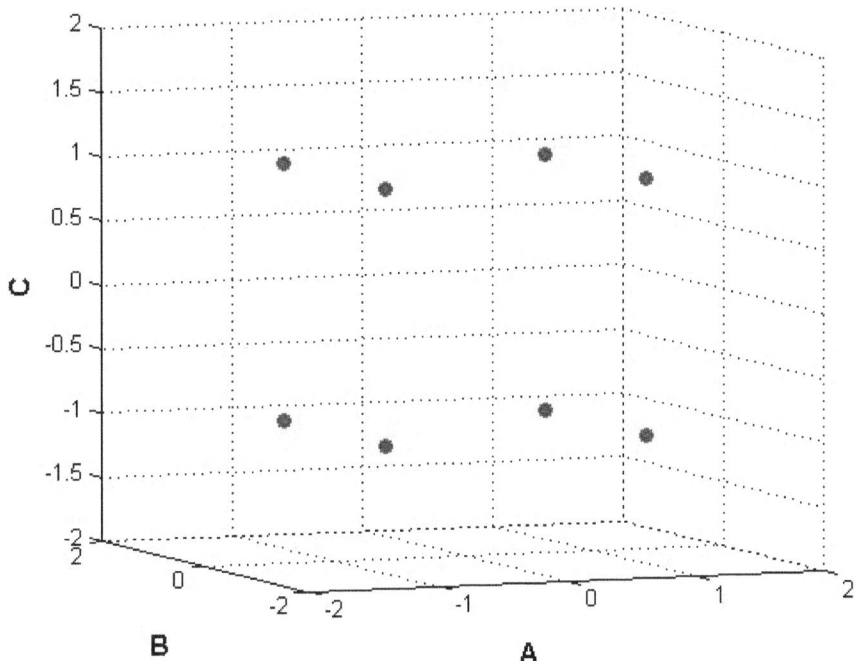

Figure 22. Graphic of a 2^3 design for factors A,B and C presented in coded space.

The CCD in Figure 23 is often referred to as a Circumscribed CCD since the factorial design portion is circumscribed within the axial runs. Other variations of the CCD are the Inscribed and Face-Centered CCDs. The Inscribed design moves the axial points inside the factorial design space and Face-Centered design moves the axial runs to the edge of the factorial design space. These designs are summarized in Tables 5 and 6 and Figures 24 and 25, respectively. Each of these CCDs are considered in Section 5.4

5.2.3 Maximum-Entropy Space Filling Design.

The final design considered is a space filling design and in particular a Maximum-Entropy Space Filling Design. "Space-filling designs are often thought to be particularly appropriate for deterministic computer models because in general they spread design points out nearly evenly or uniformly throughout the region of experimenta-

Table 4. Circumscribed Central Composite Design for Two Factors

A	B
-1	-1
-1	1
1	-1
1	1
-1.4142	0
1.4142	0
0	-1.4142
0	1.4142
0	0
0	0
0	0
0	0

Table 5. Face Centered Central Composite Design for Two Factors

A	B
-1	-1
-1	1
1	-1
1	1
-1	0
1	0
0	-1
0	1
0	0
0	0
0	0
0	0

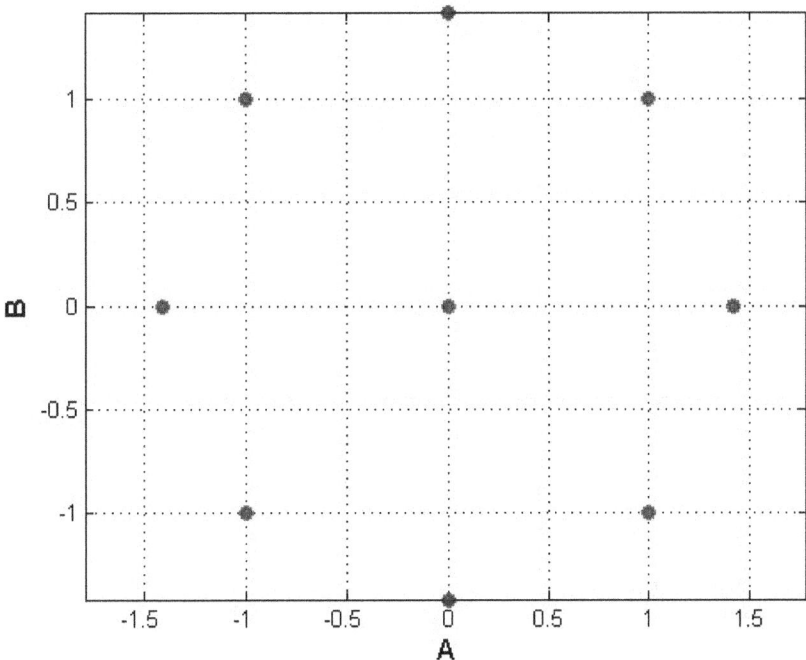

Figure 23. Graphic of a CCD with two factors in coded space. Note the spherical shape implied by the points.

tion" [38]. Even for a stochastic model, the type of model considered in this paper, the uniform spacing aspect of these experimental designs can prove to be useful. The stochastic element can be dealt with by running multiple simulations at each design point and then bootstrapping the results [24].

A popular space filling design is the Latin Hypercube. The Latin Hypercube randomly sets specific levels for a variable within defiend bands for each variable [38]. This method might not distribute the runs evenly across the design space producing gaps. The Maximum-Entropy Space Filling design was selected. This design uses design points that maximize the entropy. [38] [22] "Entropy can be thought of as a measure of the amount of information contained in the distribution of a data set." [38].

Table 6. Inscribed Central Composite Design for Two Factors

A	B
-0.7071	-0.7071
-0.7071	0.7071
0.7071	-0.7071
0.7071	0.7071
-1	0
1	0
0	-1
0	1
0	0
0	0
0	0
0	0

5.3 Interpolation Techniques

Experimental design provides a way to sample from different points within the input parameter space to achieve some defined experimental goals. However, truly testing the design space coverage requires some sort of interpolation beyond the actual design input, but still within the design space. While fairly routine with most metamodeling approaches, this becomes especially difficult when dealing with BNs and DBNs. Typically a design space is fit to different input parameters with a small number output parameters. In the case of DBNs, however, the output is an entire DBN at each design input. These DBNs are combined to produce a DBN covering the design space. DBNs typically have discrete output and often this discretization covers fixed values instead of intervals, implying that values between the bins of the discretized DBNs are not included in the DBNs and therefore require estimation. Work has been done to create continuous DBNs, but these typically assume a Gaussian distribution at each node, which is not always the case [21]. Some method is needed to interpolate between the discretized values of DBNs. This method will not produce an entirely new DBN, but simply provide an estimate of the probability in

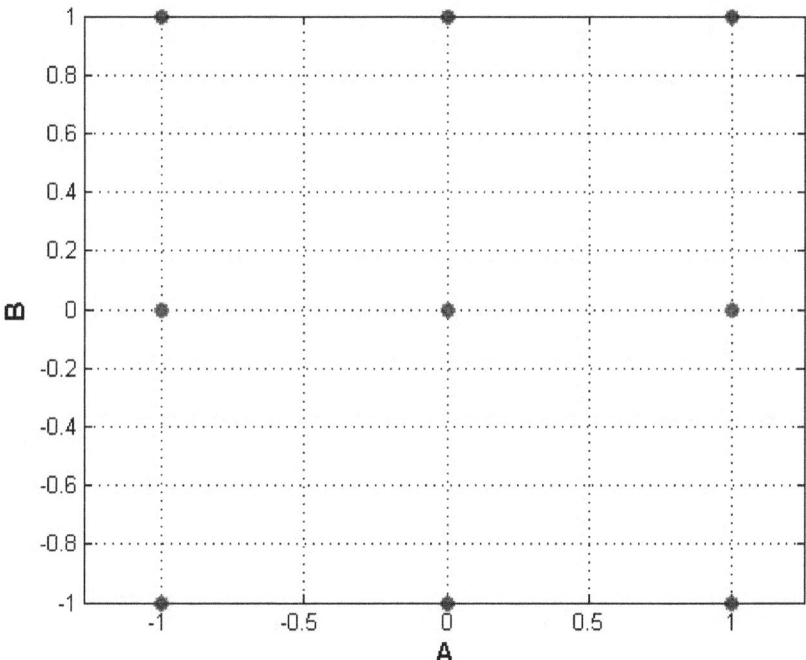

Figure 24. Graphic of a Face-Centered CCD with two factors in coded space.

question for some set of inputs. This result suffices for analytical purposes. Two methods of interpolation are compared, the first currently available and the second developed in this work.

5.3.1 Lagrange Interpolating Polynomial.

The first interpolation method is a first order Lagrange interpolating polynomial proposed by Poropudas in [48]. Let $R(X_n)$ be the set of possible design points such that $x_n \in R(X_n)$ and $R^C(X_n)$ the complement of $R(X_n)$ such that $R(X_n) \cap R^C(X_n) = \varnothing$. Now, for $x_n^* \in R^C(X_n)$, Poropudas interpolates the probability of some observation, y_m at x_n^*, as $\hat{p}(y_m|x_n^*)$ defined by Equation 5.2 [52].

$$\hat{p}(y_m|x_n) := \frac{1}{d(\underline{x}_n, \bar{x}_n)} \Sigma_{\xi=\underline{x}_n}^{\bar{x}_n} (d(\underline{x}_n, \bar{x}_n) - d(x_n, \xi)) p(y_m|\xi), \qquad (5.2)$$

69

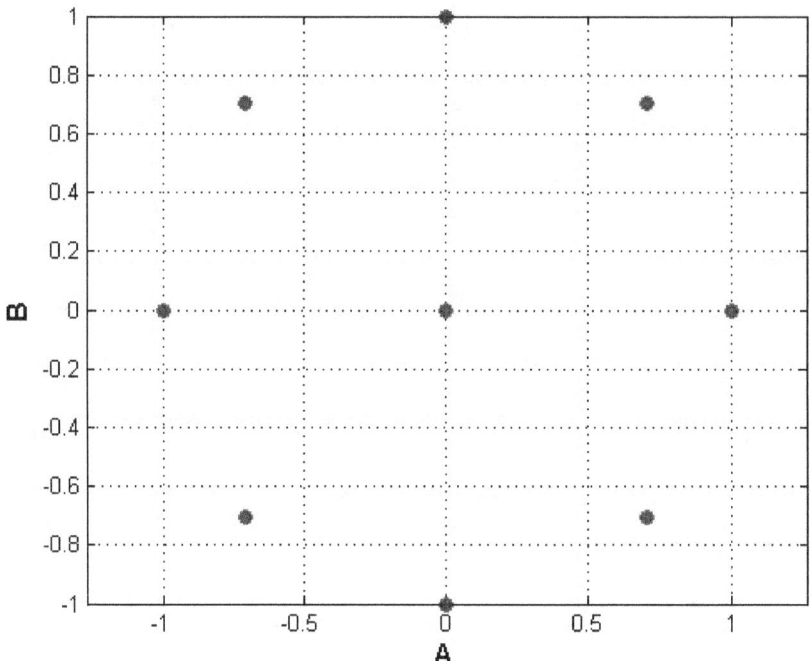

Figure 25. Graphic of an Inscribed CCD with two factors in coded space. Note the factorial portion is inscribed within the $[-1,1]$ range on each axis.

where

$$\underline{x}_n = max\{x \epsilon R(X_n) | x \leq x_n\},$$

$$\bar{x}_n = min\{x \epsilon R(X_n) | x \geq x_n\},$$

(5.3)

$d(x, y)$ is the distance between x and y defined as $d(x, y) := |x - y|$. Notice that Equation 5.2 only considers one input variable. This equation can be extended to multiple input parameters such as is shown for two parameters in Equation 5.4 [52]

$$\hat{p}(y_m | x_n, x_{n'}) := \frac{1}{d(\underline{x}_n, \bar{x}_n) d(\underline{x}_{n'}, \bar{x}_{n'})} \Sigma_{\xi' = \underline{x}_{n'}}^{\bar{x}_{n'}} \Sigma_{\xi = \underline{x}_n}^{\bar{x}_n} \left(d(\underline{x}_{n'}, \bar{x}_{n'}) \right)$$

(5.4)

$$-d(x_{n'}, \xi'))(d(\underline{x}_n, \bar{x}_n) - d(x_n, \xi))p(y_m | \xi, \xi'),$$

70

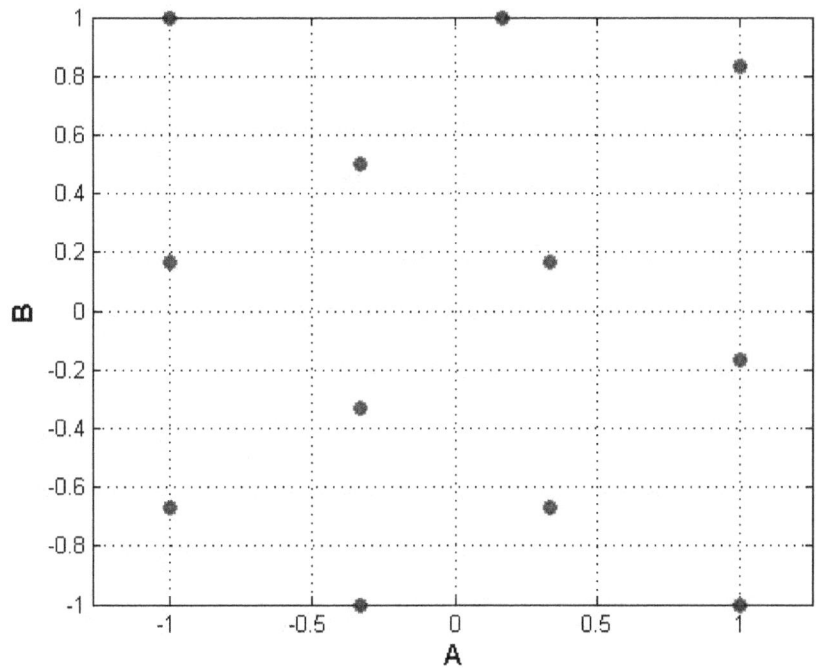

Figure 26. 12 Run Maximum-Entropy Space Filling Design with two factors

This method is a weighted sum of the probabilities with inputs closest to the inputs of the probability in question and the weights being the normalized distances between inputs.

5.3.2 Linear Regression Interpolation.

We propose a new interpolation method. This interpolation method uses linear regression techniques to provide an estimate. Suppose you have a $n \times 1$ vector of responses, $\mathbf{Y}$ corresponding to a $n \times m$ matrix of inputs $\mathbf{X}$ with the first column in $\mathbf{X}$ being a column of ones. This column of ones is necessary to estimate the response $\mathbf{Y}^*$ when the inputs $x_{i,j} = 0 \ \forall \ i, j$. These variables are related through a $m \times 1$ vector of parameters, β, and a $n \times 1$ vector, ε, of normal random variables with mean zero.

71

The variables are linearly related as defined in Equation 5.5 [29]

$$\mathbf{Y}_{n \times 1} = \mathbf{X}_{n \times m} \times \beta_{m \times 1} + \varepsilon_{n \times 1} \tag{5.5}$$

Thus, Equation 5.5 is a linear model between unknown outputs, $\mathbf{Y}$, and m variables, $\mathbf{X}$, with random error, ε. When the expected value of Equation 5.5 is taken, the random vector drops out of the equation since it is centered at 0, and $\mathbf{Y}$ can be estimated as a linear relationship of parameter estimates, β^*, and known input variables $\mathbf{X}$ [29].

$$\mathbf{Y}^* = \mathbf{X} \times \beta^*. \tag{5.6}$$

Using matrix operations, the parameter values, β^*, can now be estimated. [29]

$$\beta^* = (\mathbf{X'X})^{-1}(\mathbf{X'})\mathbf{Y}^* \tag{5.7}$$

The estimates from Equation 5.7 are used to calculate $\hat{\mathbf{Y}}$ given some input vector $\hat{\mathbf{X}}$. To account for possible non-linearities in the input space, more columns can be added to $\mathbf{X}$ to include interactions between the m variables as well as inputs that might be quadratic, cubic, etc.

For this paper the output vector $\mathbf{Y}$ is a vector of probabilities calculated from the DBN being considered and the input matrix $\mathbf{X}$ is one of the design matrices discussed in section 5.2.

5.4 Analytical Methodology

A simple M/M/1 queuing model is implemented to test the DOE and interpolation techniques proposed. The queue is a single server queue with mean service rate μ ϵ [2.5, 3] and mean interarrival rate λ ϵ [1.5, 2]. To approximate steady state, the queue is initialized with one customer in service and one in the queue. This analysis examines the number of customers in system, L_T for a given time step $T \, \epsilon \, 0, 1, 2, ..., 10$ From the parameter spaces defined for λ and μ corresponding designs are developed. The Maximum-Entropy Space Filling design with 12 runs is pictured in Figure 26, using the coded space.

Before comparing design spaces, an optimal bootstrap sample size is determined. Poropudas develops a lower bound, $\mathcal{N}$ for the number of simulation runs necessary to fit a BN given a desired significance level α [49] [52]

$$\mathcal{N} \geq z_{1-\alpha/2}^2/(4 \cdot f \cdot r^2) \tag{5.8}$$

with f defined as the least likely combination of values across all variables in the DBN and is predetermined by the user and r is the half-length from the confidence interval defined by Equation 5.9 [52]:

$$\hat{\tau} \pm z_{\alpha/2}\sqrt{Var(\hat{\tau})} \tag{5.9}$$

τ is the estimate for the probability under consideration, $P(\mathbf{A} = \mathbf{a}|\mathbf{B} = \mathbf{b})$, and $Var(\tau) = \tau(1-\tau)/\mathcal{N}_b$. $\mathcal{N}_b$ is the number of replications such that $\mathbf{B} = \mathbf{b}$. Note, that f, α and r are predetermined by the analyst, making this lower bound subjective. When $\alpha = 0.05$, $f = 0.05$ and $r = 0.05$, the lower bound comes out to be 7683.2, which past research typically tounds to 10,000. Depending on how you interpret Equation 5.8 as it relates to the number of design points, one could say that $\mathcal{N}$ is the lower bound for the number of necessary simulation runs per design point or for the entire design space. We will consider DBNs fit from 10,000 simulated runs distributed over all the design points to be "ground truth" when compared to DBNs learned from bootstrapped data.

Prior work established the viability of using bootstrapping to reduce the actual number of simulation runs needed [24]. That work involved a single data point. We next extend that work to an experimental design setting and start by determining the sample size from which to bootstrap

First, DBNs are built from 10,000 simulation runs divided evenly over the design points given by the experimental design. For example, the CCD requires 12 design points meaning each point gets $10,000 \div 12 = \lceil 833.333 \rceil = 834$, simulation runs. To determine which bootstrap sample size will produce a DBN significatnly close to the "ground truth" DBN, various bootstrap sample sizes, b are tested. [24] found that a bootstrap sampel size of 1,500 with a significance level of 0.01, would produce a suitable DBN, based on a single design point. For this paper, bootstrap sample sizes $b \epsilon \{500, 800, 1100, 1400, 1700, 2000, 2300, 2600, 2900, 3200, 3500\}$ are examined. As in [24] the Kolmogorov-Smirnov goodness of fit test (KS) is used to determine if the "ground-truth" and bootstrapped DBNs are sufficiently equivalent. For 1,000 replications the KS test statistic is calculated at each design point for each time step, t, in the DBN. A simple first order polynomial is fit to these design points using Linear Regression techniques, with the average test statistic over all 1,000 replications being the response. The response surface for each design space and bootstrap sample size is then plotted for each time step. Figures 27 - 29 are a few examples. The flat planes in each figure, represent the critical value of the KS test for a given alpha. If the response falls below some plane, then it is assumed that the bootstrap sample size produces a significant DBN for that α or smaller. Tables 7 - 9 summarize the results for all time steps and design spaces. To understand the tables, consider Table 8. For a 12 run Maximum-Entropy Space Filling Design and $\alpha = 0.1$, a bootstrap sample size of 800 is needed to ensure that all time steps, t_i, will pass the KS test. Examining

Table 7. Minimum Necessary Bootstrap Sample Size, b, necessary to pass KS Test given α, t_i and an 8 Run Maximum-Entropy Space Filling Design

8 run Maximum-Entropy Design						
	α					
Time	0.1	0.05	0.025	0.01	0.005	0.001
T0	500	500	500	500	500	500
T1	800	800	500	500	500	500
T2	800	500	500	500	500	500
T3	800	500	500	500	500	500
T4	800	500	500	500	500	500
T5	800	500	500	500	500	500
T6	500	500	500	500	500	500
T7	800	500	500	500	500	500
T8	500	500	500	500	500	500
T9	500	500	500	500	500	500
T10	500	500	500	500	500	500

Table 8. Minimum Necessary Bootstrap Sample Size, b, necessary to pass KS Test given α, t_i and an 12 Run Maximum-Entropy Space Filling Design

12 run Maximum-Entropy Design						
	α					
Time	0.1	0.05	0.025	0.01	0.005	0.001
T0	500	500	500	500	500	500
T1	800	800	500	500	500	500
T2	800	500	500	500	500	500
T3	800	500	500	500	500	500
T4	800	500	500	500	500	500
T5	800	500	500	500	500	500
T6	800	500	500	500	500	500
T7	500	500	500	500	500	500
T8	500	500	500	500	500	500
T9	500	500	500	500	500	500
T10	500	500	500	500	500	500

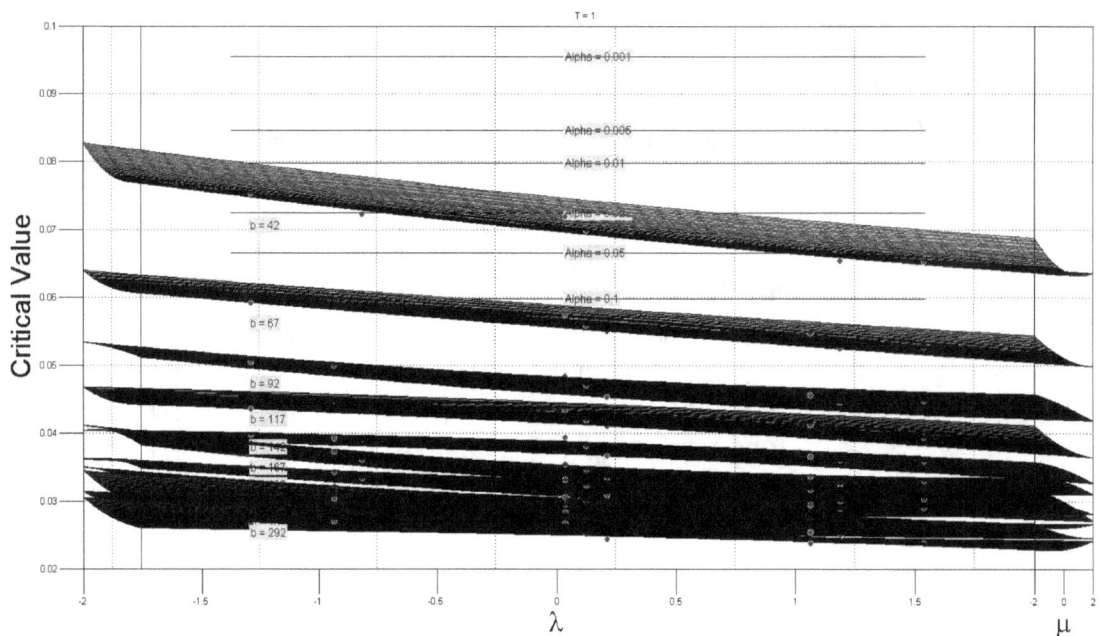

Figure 27. Average KS Test Statistic 2nd-Order Response Surface for a CCD with $T = 1$ **and Different Bootstrap Sample Sizes**

each table, we determine that a bootstrap sample size of 500 produces a suitable DBN at a significance level of 0.01.

Having settled on a bootstrap sample size of 500, the designs are next compared to see which design provides better interpolation and which interpolation technique provides better estimates.

For each experimental design under consideration a DBN is fit to each design point by bootstrapping $500/n$ simulation runs for n design points. These DBNs are combined to form one DBN for the design space. Next, a time step, t_i^*, and number in system, $L_{t_i}^*$, for that time step are chosen at random as well as a value for λ and μ, λ^* and μ^*, such that λ^* and μ^* are not a design point. $10,000/n$ simulation runs are used to estimate the true probability, $P(L_{t_i} = L_{t_i}^* | \lambda^*, \mu^*)$, and its corresponding confidence interval from Equation 5.9. Each interpolation method is used to estimate the probability $P(L_{t_i} = L_{t_i}^* | \lambda^*, \mu^*)$ and determine if it falls in the confidence interval

76

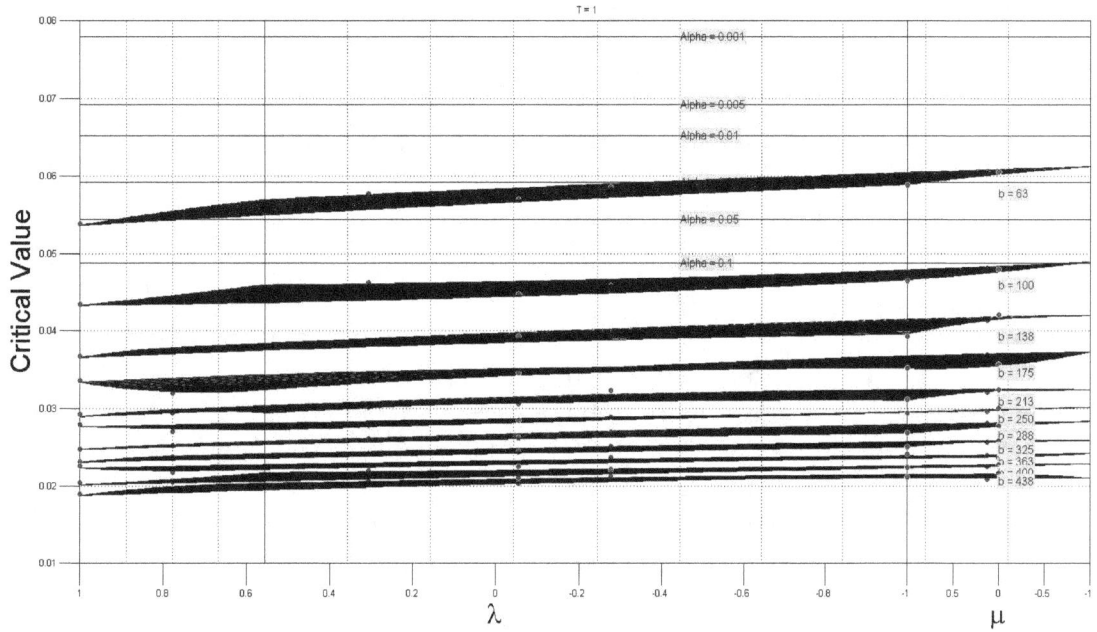

Figure 28. Average KS Test Statistic 2nd-Order Response Surface for an 8 Run Maximum-Entropy Space Filling Design with $T = 1$ and Different Bootstrap Sample Sizes

from the ground truth estimate determined from the $10,000/n$ runs. This process is repeated 1,000 times in determining the coverage or percentage of estimates that lie within their respective confidence intervals. Table 10 outlines the notation used for each design space and interpolation method. Table 11 summarizes the performance of each interpolation method.

5.5 Results

From Figures 27 - 29 and Tables 7 - 9, it appears that a bootstrap sample size of 500 is sufficient to produce significant results for a $\alpha = 0.01$. It is interesting that these results are considerably better than those in [24], which indicated a bootstrap sample size of 1,500 is sufficient. Note that in [24] the KS test was performed and the average acceptance rate of the replicated results summarized. In this paper, the KS

Table 9. Minimum Necessary Bootstrap Sample Size, b, necessary to pass KS Test given α, t_i and an Circumscribed Central Composite Design

Circumscribed Central Composite Design						
	α					
Time	0.1	0.05	0.025	0.01	0.005	0.001
T0	500	500	500	500	500	500
T1	800	800	800	500	500	500
T2	800	800	500	500	500	500
T3	800	500	500	500	500	500
T4	800	500	500	500	500	500
T5	800	500	500	500	500	500
T6	800	500	500	500	500	500
T7	800	500	500	500	500	500
T8	500	500	500	500	500	500
T9	800	500	500	500	500	500
T10	500	500	500	500	500	500

Table 10. Design and Interpolation Notation Key

Key
L = 1st-Order Lagrange Interpolation Polynomial
P_1 = 1st-Order Polynomial
P_2 = 2nd-Order Polynomial
P_3 = 3rd-Order Polynomial
CCD_C = Circumscribed Central Composite Design
CCD_F = Face-centered Central Composite Design
CCD_I = Inscripbed Central Composite Design
ME_8 = 8 Run Maximum-Entropy Space Filling Design
ME_{12} = 12 Run Maximum-Entropy Space Filling Design
FF = Full Factorial DesignDesign

Table 11. Interpolation Coverage for Each Experimental Design and Interpolation Method

	Experimental Design					
Interpolation	CCD_C	CCD_F	CCD_I	ME_8	ME_{12}	FF
L	39%	-	-	25.00%	18%	52.00%
P_1	59.5	76.40%	63.30%	60.00%	73.30%	50.40%
P_2	51.80%	58.20%	52.80%	54%	50.60%	-
P_3	-	-	-	-	45.50%	-

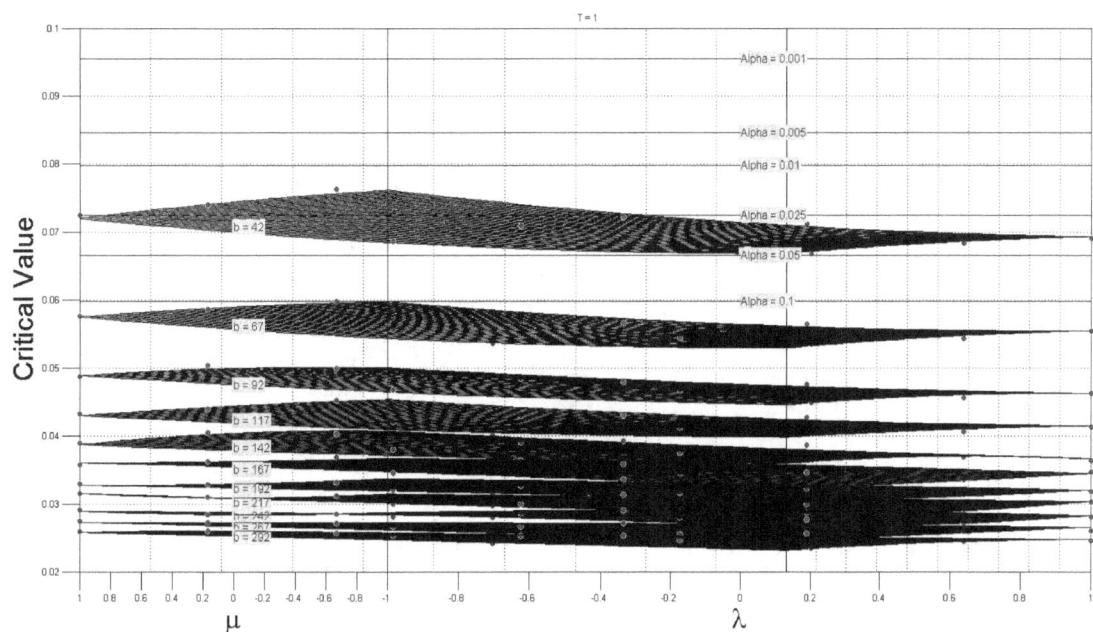

Figure 29. Average KS Test Statistic 2nd-Order Response Surface for an 12 Run Maximum-Entropy Space Filling Design with $T = 1$ and Different Bootstrap Sample Sizes

test statistic is averaged across all replications and it is this value that is used in the goodness of fit test as seen in Figures 27 - 29. This implies that the average KS test statistic for low bootstrap sample sizes is small enough to pass the KS test, however when compared individually a larger percentage of the KS test statistics imply failure, but they are small enough not to effect the average of the test statistic and therefore close to passing the KS test.

The interpolation method comparisons are also compared using a bootstrap sample size of 500. Theses results, summarized in Table 11, indicate that using a Face-Centered Central Composite Design and a simple first-order polynomial produce the best results.

Since the Face-Centered Central Composite Design and Space Filling Design with 12 runs produce roughly similar results and the Space Filling Design with 8 runs uses fewer design points, further analysis is performed on these designs. The First-Order

Polynomial interpolation test was repeated for each of these designs 100 times testing 1,000 points for each replication. The results are summarized in Table 12 indicating that the 12 run Maximum-Entropy Space Filling design performs the best.

Table 12. First-Order Linear Regression Interpolation Coverage for Multiple Designs over 100 Replications

	Experimental Design		
Interpolation	CCD_F	ME_8	ME_{12}
P_1	66.34%	59.46%	68.69%

The interpolation results are considerably better than the current Lagrange Interpolating Polynomial method for all design spaces except in the Full Factorial space. The results also indicate that a Space Filling design or Face Centered Central Composite design produce better results than the Full Factorial design.

Finally, for further exploration, a first-order polynomial fit to a Maximum-Entropy Space Filling Design with 12 design points was constructed for bootstrap sample sizes $b \in \{500, 800, 1100, 1400, 1700, 2000, 2300, 2600, 2900, 3200, 3500\}$. The coverage was then checked across 1,000 test points at each bootstrap sample size.

Table 13. Interpolation Coverage at varying Bootstrap Sample Sizes for fixed α

Bootstrap Sample Size	CI Coverage
500	68.69%
800	73.10%
1100	77.70%
1400	78.70%
1700	78.70%
2000	78.70%
2300	77.10%
2600	80.00%
2900	78.00%
3200	78.50%
3500	79.40%

The results indicate that increasing the bootstrap sample size improves the coverage up to a bootstrap sample size of 1,100 and then effectively levels off. For future work the effects of increasing bootstrap sample size should be compared to the effects of increasing the number of design points.

5.6 Conclusions

DBNs have been proposed as useful metamodels for simulations, however, they require too much data for any practical results. We reduce the number of runs necessary utilizing bootstrapping techniques. Past work focused on a single design point or a single dimension. This work extended DBN use to the full design space by examining potential experimental designs. Finally, the available interpolation method does not perform well. We propose and test a vastly improved method. Collectively these contributions establish the viability of DBNs for practical metamodeling use and analytical insight.

There is still plenty of work needed to continue developing DBNs as metamodels. Three major design spaces were considered in this paper, but there are many more that can be tested. Simple Linear Regression equations were proposed as an alternative interpolation method, but other methods should be explored to find a more effective technique. The relationship between number of bootstrap samples and the coverage of the confidence intervals poses an interesting question. Finally, only a two dimension experimental design was considered. Future research should consider higher dimensional response surface designs.

DBNs as metamodels for simulations is a new area that still requires further research, however, this paper offers some techniques to reduce the number of simulation runs necessary to fit a DBN to the simulation and introduces new more effective interpolation techniques to explore points within the design space of the DBN.

VI. Case Study

6.1 Introduction

In the defense world, decision makers are faced with many different combat situations for which they have to be best prepared. They are constantly working to understand the battle as much as possible before it happens and attempt to create an efficient tool for real-time analysis during the conflict. Bayesian Networks (BN) are graphical models that relate variables probabilistically. The conditional independence relationships in BNs allow for information to be passed quickly through the network and offers efficient "what-if" analysis. Dynamic Bayesian Netowrks (DBN) are simply BNs carried through time and therefore allow the modeler to capture the time aspect present in many combat situations. For these reasons, we argue that DBNs should be used as metamodels for current combat simulations. The goal of this case study is to present Dynamic Bayesian Networks (DBN) as suitable metamodels for combat simulations to be used for probabilistic analysis now and quick real-time combat analysis in preparation for any event during a conflict. The rest of this study is outlined as follows. Section 2 describes the combat model used to generate data for the DBN. Section 3 outlines the methodology for fitting a DBN to simulated data. Sections 4 and 5 present the results and analysis of the DBN metamodel, respectively. Section 6 is a conclusion of the case study.

6.2 Combat Simulation

To illustrate metamodeling combat models with DBNs, the following mission level model is presented. Suppose there is a threat of a Blue Air Force (AF) base being attacked by 16 red cruise missile launchers. The base is defended by 4 F-16s, two of which are equipped with sensors and the other two with missiles. These fighters circle the base sensing incoming cruise missiles and then firing upon them when they come within in a certain range, R. Each blue missile has some probability of kill, P_k. The cruise missile launchers are stationed some distance from the AF base outside the range of the F-16 missiles. The base is unaware if fired upon until the red missile enters the sensor range. Once the cruise missiles have been detected, their location information is constantly passed to the F-16s equipped with weapons systems, which then attempt to shoot down the cruise missiles when they enter the fighters range. This combat situation was modeled using the System Effectiveness Analysis Simulation (SEAS) [35] [14]. A picture of the situation is shown in Figure 30. The decision maker is interested in the number of cruise missiles that make it through the defenses and hit the base. Cruise missiles that hit the base are referred to as leaks. In particular, how does the current blue missile technology perform against incoming cruise missiles or more specifically how does the probability of kill and range of the blue missiles effect the outcome of the conflict. The decision makers wish to know what the average number of leaks and hits are for the given situation, the uncertainty surrounding these averages and how these averages and this uncertainty are effected by changes in the current technology.

6.3 Methodology

To metamodel the situation described in Section 6.1 with a DBN and provide sufficient analysis, it is necessary to run the simulation at various input parameters and for each set of input parameters a large number of simulation runs are needed to account for the stochasticity of the model. Poropudasand Virtanen [49] provide a lower bound for the number of simulation runs needed to fit a DBN,

$$\mathcal{N} \geq z^2_{1-\alpha/2}/(4 \cdot f \cdot r^2). \tag{6.1}$$

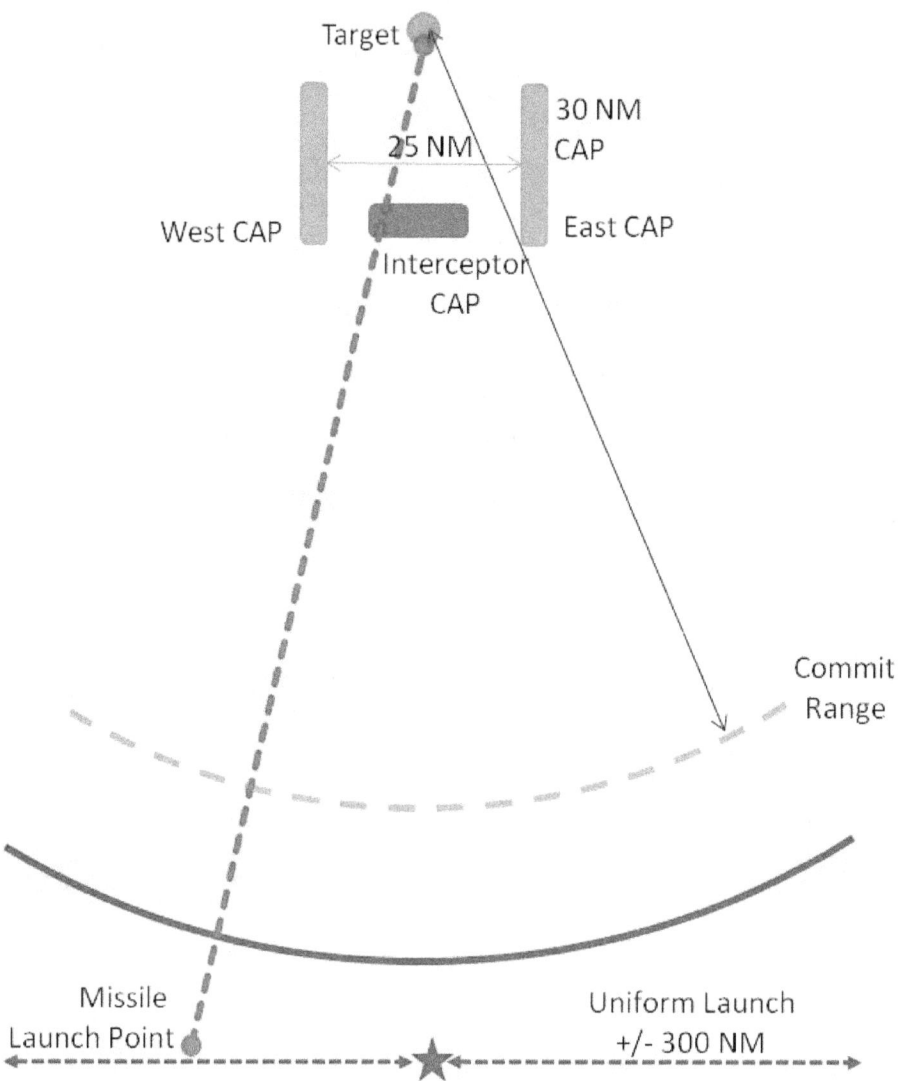

Figure 30. Combat situation modeled in SEAS [35] [14].

In Equation 6.1, f is the probability of the least likely combination of certain values for each of the variables in the DBN and r is the desired half-width of the confidence interval, Equation 6.3, for each probability in the DBN. f and r are predefined by the decision maker.

Setting $\alpha = 0.05$, $f = 0.05$ and $r = 0.05$ yields a lower bound of 7,683.2 simulation runs needed to fit a DBN. Rounding up gives 10,000 simulation runs. For the SEAS model in this study 10,000 simulation runs would take a couple of days and require considerable computer power, but is feasible. 10,000 simulation runs, however, is not very feasible for campaign level combat models especially if the decision makers wish to gain insight on various combat situations running many different models. How then do we reduce the number of runs necessary to fit the DBN while still providing sufficient probabilistic insight into the outcome of the situation and spanning the input parameter space under consideration? We will reduce the number of runs using bootstrapping techniques and will cover the input parameter space using a Design of Experiment (DOE) method and interpolation techniques to make predictions within the DBN.

Based upon results from previous work [25], a 12 run Maximum-Entropy Space Filling design is chosen to cover the input parameter space with $0.7 \leq P_k \leq 0.9$ and $16 \leq R \leq 20$ The SEAS model is run at each of the design points in Figure 31,

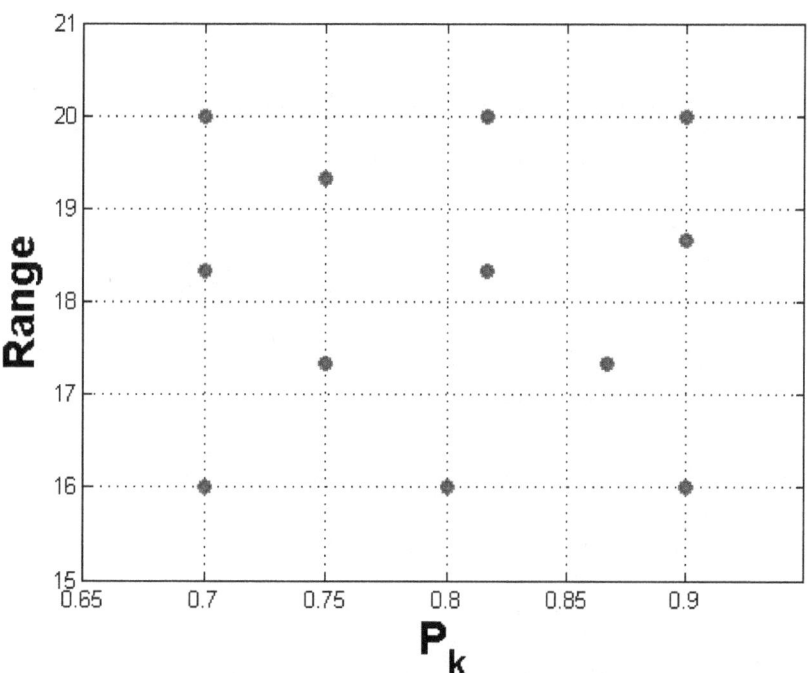

Figure 31. 12-run Maximum-Entropy Space Filling Design input parameter space.

834 times to populate a "ground-truth" DBN (10,008 total runs). Note, that each

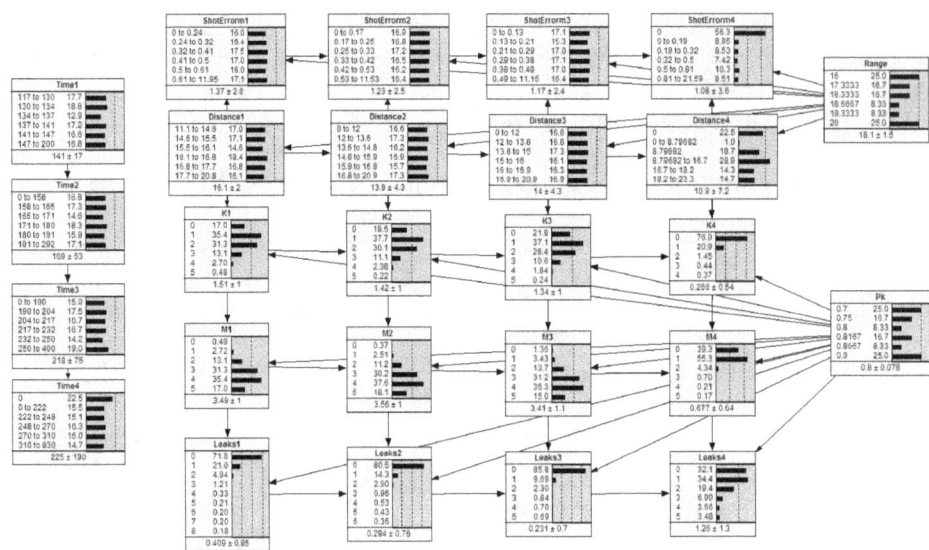

Figure 32. Ground truth Dynamic Bayesian Network fit to 10,008 simulated data points.

time step is an aggregation of 5 events occurring, events being blue shots on red or red hitting the AF base. Initially, range and probability of kill were connected to all variables in the DBN except for time. After further examination it was determined that Range does not have a significant effect on misses, kills and leaks and what effect it does have can be transmitted through the arcs connecting shot error and distance to misses, kills or leaks. The same is true for probability of kill, but in relation to distance and shot error. Next, the first $\lceil b/12 \rceil$ samples are taken from the simulated data at each design point for $b \in \{500, 1100, 3000\}$. These sample sizes were determined in previous work [24] [25]. For each sample size, b, the removed sample is bootstrapped [13] to produce 834 data points for each design point. This bootstrapped data is used to fit a DBN that is then compared to the "ground-truth" DBN using the 2-sample Kolmogorov-Smirnov (KS) goodness of fit test with an alpha of 0.01. Figures 33 - 35 are the DBNs learned from bootstrapped data.

Next, an interpolation technique is used to estimate the probability of events occurring that are within the input parameter design space, but not at the actual

86

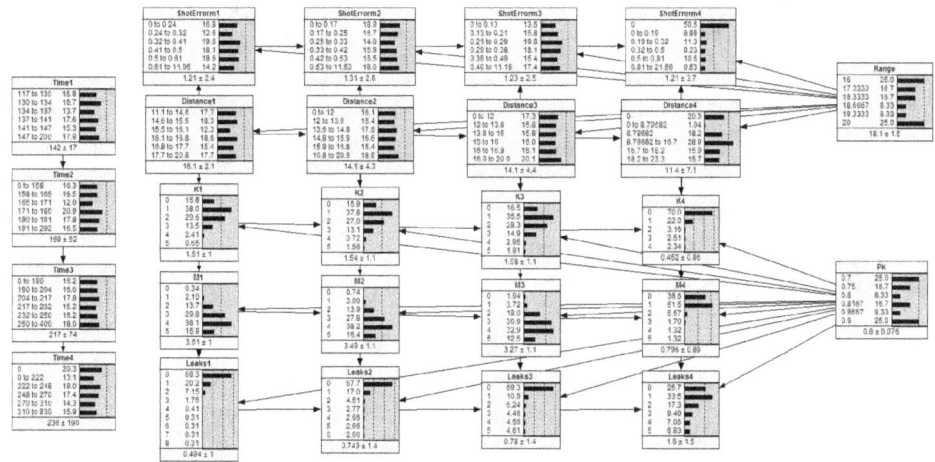

Figure 33. Dynamic Bayesian Network fit to bootstrapped data with bootstrap sample size $b = 500$.

design points and therefore not included in the DBN. This interpolation allows the decision maker to estimate the probability of a certain number of leaks occurring given a P_k and R between the discretized bins present in DBNs. The interpolation method uses linear regression to fit a first-order polynomial to the input parameter design points. The output for each design point is a probability specified by the decision maker and estimated from the bootstrapped DBN. For example, suppose the decision maker wants an interpolation estimate for the probability that the number of leaks at time step 3 is 1, given $P_k = 0.73$ and $R = 16.75$, $P(Leaks_3 = 1|P_k = 0.73, R = 16.75)$. The interpolation function for $P(L_3 = 1|P_k, R)$ is derived from the bootstrapped DBN for all design points using linear regression. Equation 6.2 is defined by fitting column 3 in Table 14 to columns 1 and 2 using the method of least squares.

$$P(L_3 = 1|P_k, R) = 0.3183 - 0.3184 * P_k + 0.001709 * R \qquad (6.2)$$

Then, setting $P_k = 0.73$ and $R = 16.75$ in Equation 6.2 returns a probability estimate of 0.1145 and the decision maker can infer that the probability of 1 leak at time step 3 is 11.45%.

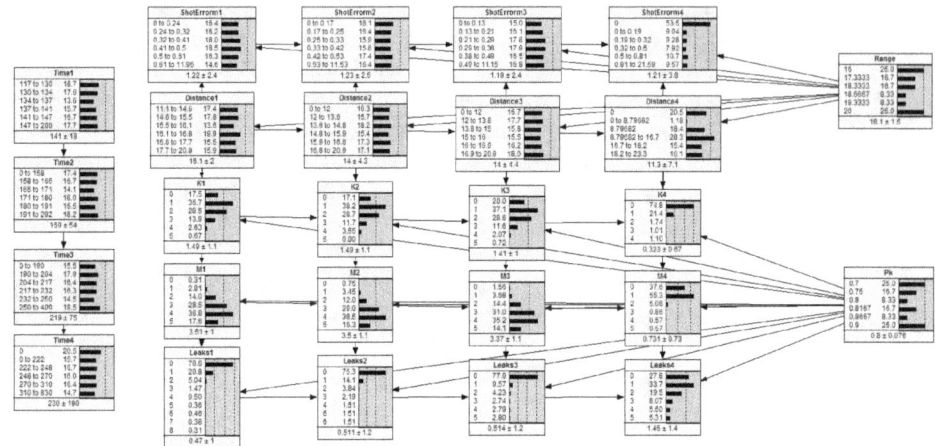

Figure 34. Dynamic Bayesian Network fit to bootstrapped data with bootstrap sample size $b = 1,100$.

Interpolation is further used to test the validity of each bootstrapped DBN, by comparing 10 random interpolation results to their ground truth probabilities and confidence intervals for the ground truth probabilities. The confidence interval used is defined in Equation 6.3 [49].

$$\hat{\tau} \pm z_{\alpha/2}\sqrt{Var(\hat{\tau})} \tag{6.3}$$

$Var(\tau) = \tau(1-\tau)/\mathcal{N}_b$ with τ being the estimate for the probability under consideration, $P(\mathbf{A} = \mathbf{a}|\mathbf{B} = \mathbf{b})$. $\mathcal{N}_b$ is the number of replications such that $\mathbf{B} = \mathbf{b}$. The test points considered in this study are summarized in Table 15.

Finally, we consider the question of what the results would look like if only the bootstrap sample is used, without bootstrapping? To answer these question the results of the KS test are paired with the confidence intervals from the data. Using Equation 6.1 we solve for r to get an expression for confidence interval half-width in terms of sample size considered, $\mathcal{N}$.

$$r = \frac{z_{1-\alpha/2}}{\sqrt{(4 \cdot \mathcal{N} \cdot f)}} \tag{6.4}$$

88

Table 14. 12 Run Maximum-Entropy Space Filling Design Inputs and Probability Outputs

P_k	R	$P(Leaks_3 = 1|P_k, R)$
0.9	20	0.0647
0.9	16	0.0624
0.7	20	0.1223
0.8167	18.3333	0.0983
0.7	18.3333	0.1079
0.75	19.3333	0.1175
0.9	18.6667	0.048
0.7	16	0.1343
0.75	17.3333	0.1127
0.8167	20	0.1127
0.8667	17.3333	0.0695
0.8	16	0.0839

Table 15. Test points used to test the interpolation method.

Test Point	P_k	R	Variable	Value/Bin
1	0.794736788	19.37322575	$Time_3$	146.16
2	0.811440969	18.32966299	$Leaks_3$	3
3	0.833726524	18.34698791	K_3	4
4	0.741094302	18.86156287	$ShotErrorm_2$	0.465826
5	0.868580536	19.20058698	M_4	1
6	0.881842583	19.77004254	$ShotErrorm_3$	0.0505016
7	0.887197605	19.26136777	$Time_2$	205.12
8	0.891250386	18.45649274	$Time_2$	164.46
9	0.760363556	19.55529691	K_2	1
10	0.864322955	19.98752608	M_1	3

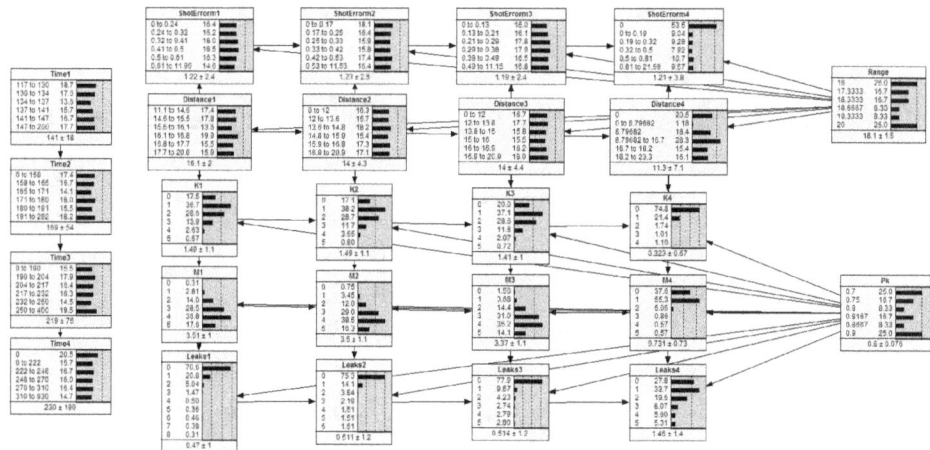

Figure 35. Dynamic Bayesian Network fit to bootstrapped data with bootstrap sample size $b = 3,000$.

If we use a bootstrap sample size of 500 without bootstrapping Equation 6.4 yields an approximate half-width of 20%. This half-width yields a very large confidence interval indicating that we cannot be very confident in our probability estimates. Using bootstrapping we can reduce the half-width size, increasing confidence and still ensure that our data comes from the same distribution as the "ground-truth" data using the KS test.

6.4 Results

Figures 36 - 38 summarize the results of the KS test. Blue indicates that the results failed the KS test and red that they passed. Thus, a bootstrap sample size of 3,000 is obviously the best choice, however, note that the results are arguably acceptable for all of the Measures of Performance (MoP) variables (Misses, Hits, Leaks) at sample size $b = 1,100$. The DBN we have presented aggregates events in the simulation, which is most likely having a significant effect on the KS results.

We now turn to the interpolation results to determine the most appropriate and efficient DBN to use. Unfortunately, due to the run time of the SEAS model, we

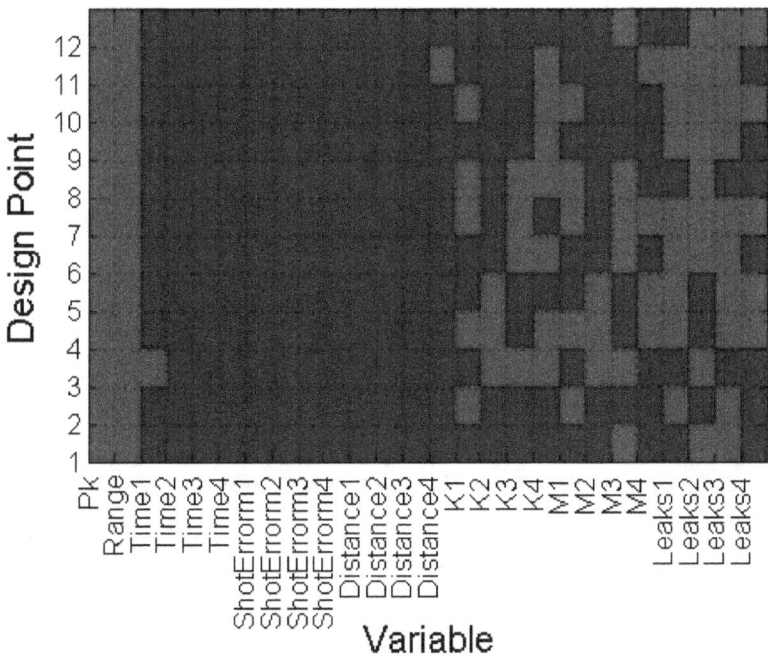

Figure 36. 2-sample Kolmogorov-Smirnov goodness of fit test results for $\alpha = 0.05$ and $b = 500$. Blue indicates that the resuls failed the test and red that it passed.

limited ourselves to testing the 10 points shown in Table 15. Ideally the interpolation coverage percentages should be tested against hundreds or even thousands of points. Table 16, however, does present the average interpolation results for 100 different replications of bootstrapped data tested against the 10 points. From Table 16 we see that even without bootstrapping, $b = 1$, the simple linear regression interpolation technique performs well under the design space. This would imply that the response

Table 16. Interpolation Coverage for Different Bootstrap Sample Sizes Tested on 10 Points

b	Interpolation Coverage
1	70.0%
100	70.0%
500	83.4%
1100	57.9%
3000	75.5%

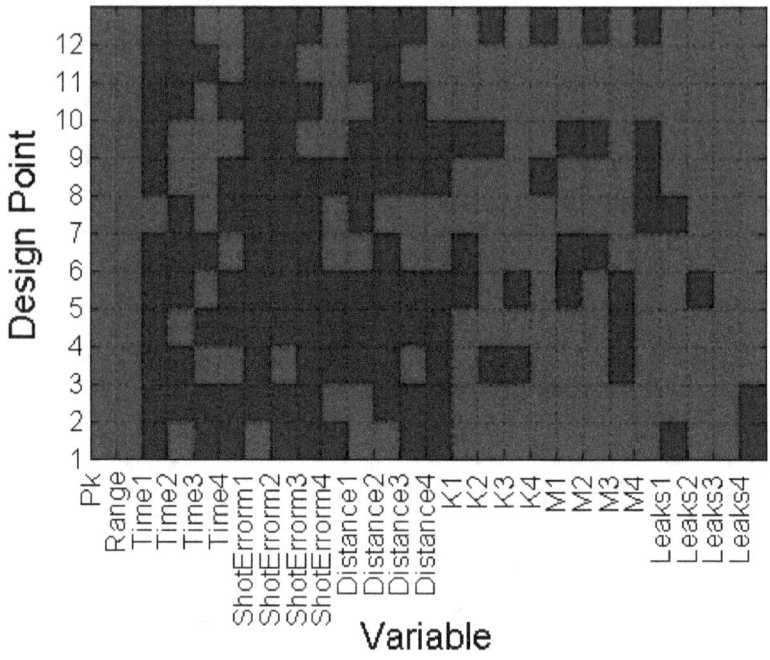

Figure 37. 2-sample Kolmogorov-Smirnov goodness of fit test results for $\alpha = 0.05$ and $b = 1,100$. Blue indicates that the resuls failed the test and red that it passed.

surface across the design space is linear, as we expected, and the randomness present in the simulation is very small.

Before concluding this case study we show how the DBNs might be used. Let's assume that we are content with the DBN built from 500 simulation runs pictured in Figure 33. We can use the DBN to perform "what-if" analysis, by putting evidence into the network. For example, suppose the decision maker wishes to know the risk of arming the F-16s with minimal performance weapons systems or missiles with probability kill, $P_k = 0.7$, and range, $R = 16$. Simply putting this evidence into the DBN updates the probabilities of the remaining variables giving mean responses as well the probability distributions across each variable or uncertainty surrounding the variables. This is shown in Figure 39, which can be compared to the original DBN in Figure 33. Various scenarios can be considered by instantiating the network with

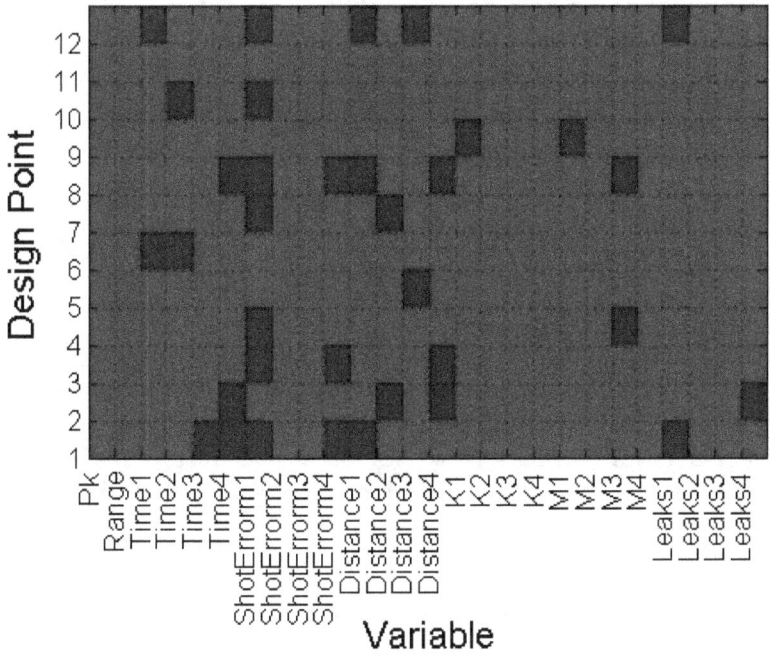

Figure 38. 2-sample Kolmogorov-Smirnov goodness of fit test results for $\alpha = 0.05$ **and** $b = 3,000$. **Blue indicates that the resuls failed the test and red that it passed.**

different evidence inputs or even sets of evidence inputs. This "what-if" analysis can be performed before a conflict arises, but due to the conditional independence properties present in DBNs quick solutions with corresponding uncertainty can also be calculated in real-time if necessary. Also, the linear regression interpolation method presented in this study can be used to extrapolate beyond the network if required. This extrapolation has not been tested and the results should be taken with extreme caution since they will lie outside the design space (as is the case with any extrapolation).

Finally, what happens if we do not bootstrap, but simply use the sample we pulled from the "ground-truth" data? The results indicate that a subset of the 10,000 point data set would always pass the KS-test. This is trivially true since the KS-test is used to determine whether or not the two data sets come from the same

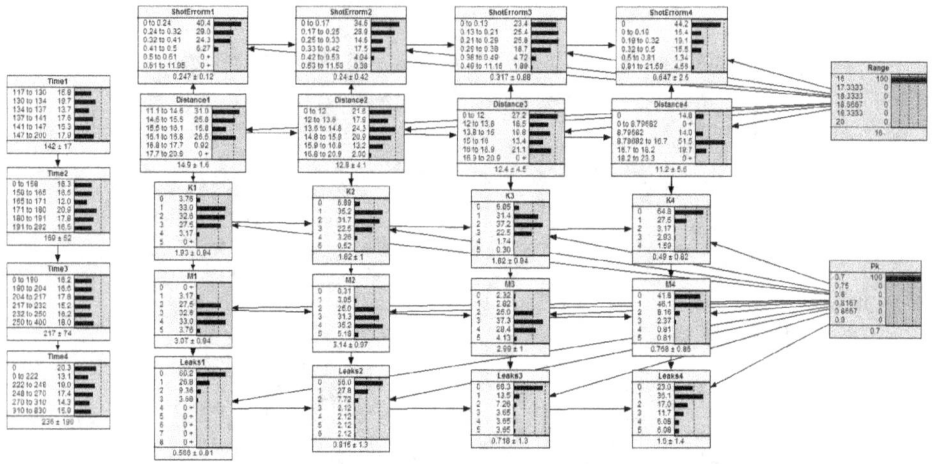

Figure 39. Dynamic Bayesian Network fit to bootstrapped data with bootstrap sample size $b = 500$. The evidence $P_k = 0.7$ and $R = 16$ has been instantiated in the network

distribution. The issue with not using bootstrapping is in the confidence of the results. Without bootstrapping the confidence intervals are exceptionally larger than with bootstrapping. Tables 17 - 19 and their respective figures, Figures 40 - 42, show the half-widths for various bootstrap sample sizes when they are bootstrapped to various augmented data sizes and when they are not bootstrapped at all. Note that these tables and figures represent the average results over all variables, time steps and design points for 10 replications. Bootstrapping is a double-edged sword. Creating more data through bootstrapping reduces the half-width of the confidence interval, but it may create a data set that is not significantly similar to the 10,000 'ground-truth" data points. This is where the KS-test is useful. If we bootstrap too much, the data set will fail the KS test implying that the bootstrapped data and "ground-truth" data do not have the same underlying distribution. Therefore bootstrapping coupled with the KS test allows us to increase our confidence in our estimates while producing a data set that is significantly similar to the "ground-truth" data set. It is up to the decision maker to determine what level of confidence and significance they desire. To achieve the best accuracy, we recommend running

94

Table 17. Average Half-widths, Probability Estimates and KS Acceptance Rate for Various Bootstrapped Data Sizes with $b = 500$ and $\alpha = 0.05$

Bootstrap Sample Size $b = 500$			
Bootstrappped Size	Average Half-Width	Average Probability	% KS Accept
500	0.286966075	0.089512918	0.983974359
1512	0.16565837	0.089534037	0.671794872
2520	0.128321051	0.08952432	0.532692308
3528	0.108451167	0.0895401	0.450641026
4536	0.09565486	0.089449022	0.398717949
5544	0.086519755	0.089489864	0.358974359
6552	0.079589027	0.089479455	0.341025641
7560	0.074094626	0.089483153	0.321794872
8568	0.069598985	0.089496966	0.312179487
9576	0.065833879	0.089498843	0.309294872
10584	0.062621388	0.089500684	0.3
11592	0.05983563	0.089525968	0.28974359
12600	0.057391889	0.089524459	0.283012821
13608	0.055226197	0.089502772	0.284615385
14616	0.053287028	0.089536032	0.282692308

Table 18. Average Half-widths, Probability Estimates and KS Acceptance Rate for Various Bootstrapped Data Sizes with $b = 1,100$ and $\alpha = 0.05$

Bootstrap Sample Size $b = 1,100$			
Bootstrappped Size	Average Half-Width	Average Probability	% KS Accept
1100	0.198742592	0.047984296	0.996794872
2208	0.140531635	0.047973946	0.857051282
3312	0.114740439	0.047985729	0.774679487
4416	0.099371131	0.047951781	0.704166667
5520	0.08887874	0.047978049	0.655769231
6624	0.081134859	0.047976332	0.616025641
7728	0.075116648	0.047994641	0.591346154
8832	0.070265192	0.047983054	0.559294872
9936	0.06624714	0.047984821	0.549038462
11040	0.062847064	0.047979498	0.533653846
12144	0.059921689	0.047998108	0.520512821
13248	0.057371976	0.047974089	0.507051282
14352	0.055120746	0.047986582	0.503846154
15456	0.053115878	0.047992643	0.473397436
16560	0.051314973	0.047979124	0.476282051

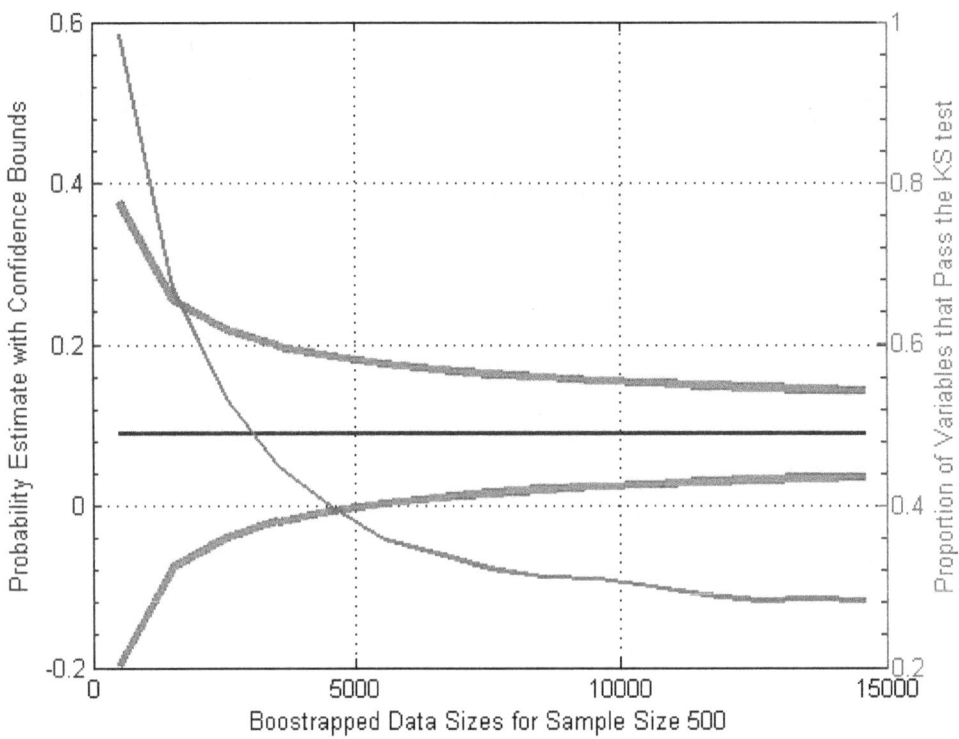

Figure 40. KS Test Acceptance Rate at $\alpha = 0.05$ and Confidence Interval Half-widths for Various Sizes of Bootstrapped Data from Sample Size $b = 500$

the simulation 3,000 times and then bootstrapping this data to approximately 10,000 data points to fit the DBN to. If, however, the decision maker cannot afford 3,000 runs then 1,100 runs bootstrapped to approximately 4,400 data points will improve the half-width of the confidence interval from 0.2 to 0.1, but the KS test will still pass 70% of the time. Bootstrapping beyond 4,400, to say 12,000, will significantly reduce the number of variables that pass the KS test, but move the half-width to 0.06 which is significantly close to the desired half-width of 0.05. Finally, if all that is available is a sample size of 500 runs, then bootstrapping this data more will move it farther away from the underlying distribution eventually failing the KS test. However, as previous work and this work indicates, our interpolation method will still offer excellent results even without bootstrapping. Bootstrapping a sample size of 500 to 2,520 data points

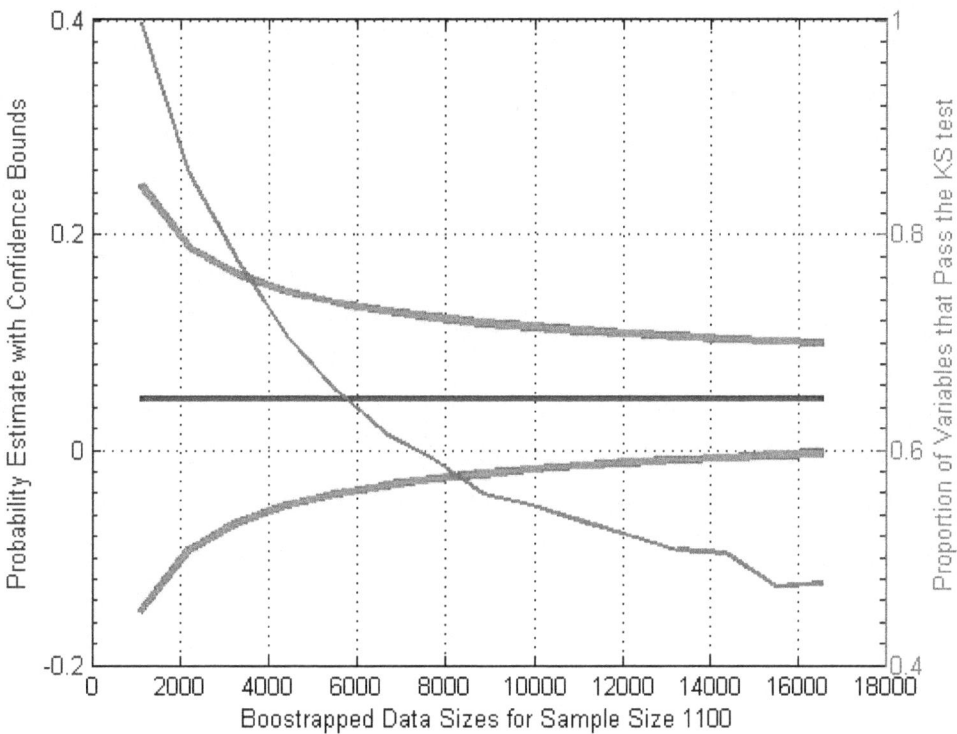

Figure 41. KS Test Acceptance Rate at $\alpha = 0.05$ and Confidence Interval Half-widths for Various Sizes of Bootstrapped Data from Sample Size $b = 1100$

will reduce the half-width to 0.13 while 53% of the variables still pass the KS test. Note that these values come from a KS test with $\alpha = 0.05$. If α is reduced to 0.01 the results will improve.

6.5 Conclusions

This case study set out to illustrate the use of DBNs as suitable metamodels for combat simulations. The results showed that, depending on the decision makers desired significance level, useful DBNs can be built from 3,000 simulation runs and arguably as little as 500. These DBNs can then be used to quickly perform "what-if" analysis, provide probability estimates of outcomes and possibly extrapolate to probability estimates outside the design space.

Table 19. Average Half-widths, Probability Estimates and KS Acceptance Rate for Various Bootstrapped Data Sizes with $b = 3,000$ and $\alpha = 0.05$

Bootstrap Sample Size $b = 3,000$			
Bootstrappped Size	Average Half-Width	Average Probability	% KS Accept
3000	0.122509728	0.020502268	1
6000	0.08662718	0.020504803	0.941666667
9000	0.070730701	0.020508392	0.905448718
12000	0.061254765	0.020498331	0.888461538
15000	0.054787775	0.020500313	0.868269231

DBNs should be considered a practical alternative to the current metamodels in use. However, there is plenty of future research needed to improve DBNs as metamodels. This paper focused on a mission level model, however, the methods presented should be further tested on campaign level models. The "ground-truth" DBN was assumed to need only 10,000 simulation runs. More analysis should be done to determine some more concrete relationship between the number of runs necessary to fit a DBN and say the number of variables present in the model. The bootstrapping technique utilized was very basic. Strategically simulating runs to bootstrap might help cover the space even better than current results. Other goodness of fit tests such as the Anderson-Darling test should be explored to see which test provides more accurate DBNs. Lastly, 500 to 3,000 may still be a considerably large number of simulation runs for some combat models. We encourage the decision makers to use the time before a conflict arises to run the combat models and create accurate DBN metamodels that can be utilized as needed in the future. This simulated data can be paired with previous runs, historical data and subject matter expertise to develop robust DBN metamodels.

There is still a lot of research to be done in improving DBN metamodeling, but this case study demonstrates the practicality and usefulness of DBNs as combat simulation metamodels. DBNs can efficiently model the time aspects present in combat

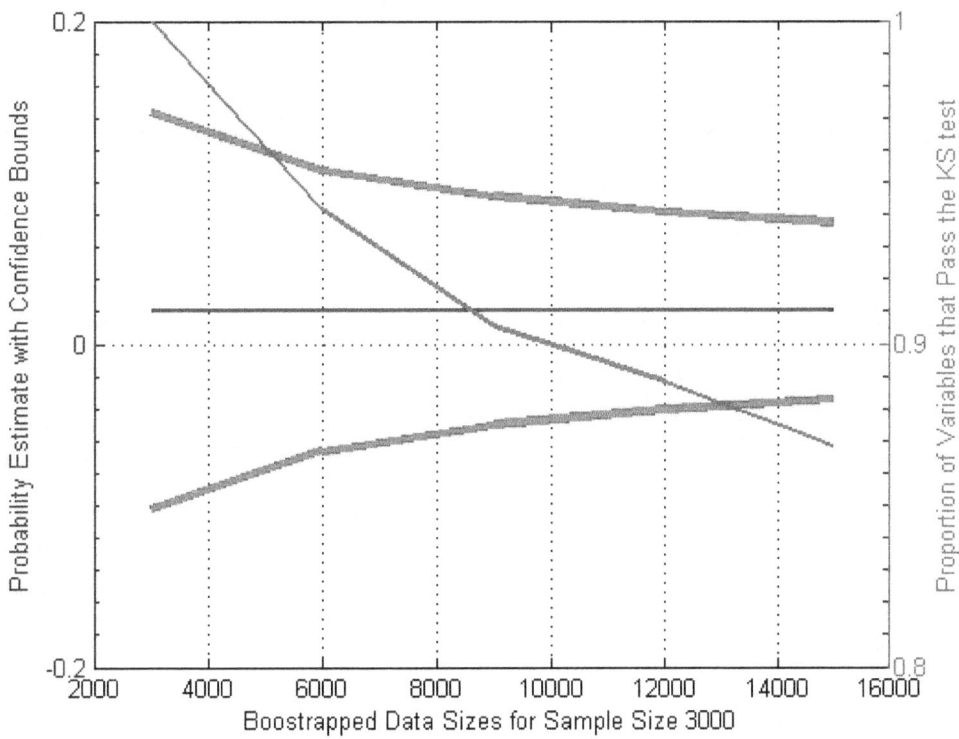

Figure 42. KS Test Acceptance Rate at $\alpha = 0.05$ **and Confidence Interval Half-widths for Various Sizes of Bootstrapped Data from Sample Size** $b = 3000$

simulations, capture the uncertainty surrounding current combat simulations and help

the analysts perform quick "what-if" analysis.

VII. Contributions and Future Research

The goal of this research is make DBNs a more practical metamodeling tool. Why DBNs? There are currently numerous metamodeling tools available, but they do not model the time aspect present in many simulations and often the standard metamodels only output a mean response. DBNs can model time and output a probability distribution of outcomes capturing the uncertainty often present in simulations. Another argument for using DBNs as metamodels is their ability to model at a higher resolution. The motivation behind this research is to provide a suitable metamodel for analyts to capture the uncertainty and perform quick "what-if" analysis on campaign level combat models. DBNs relate variables probabilistically in stead of providing an analytical solution allowing the decision maker to model at higher resolution and perform quick analysis.

7.1 Contributions

Current work in metamodeling with DBNs requires a potentially infeasible amount of simulated data to train the DBNs and then does not interpolate well within the parameter space of the network to provide specific estimates. This research successfully improved the practicality of DBNs as metamodels as well as other contributions to the Modeling and Simulation (M&S) world.

First, bootstrapping techniques and experimental designs were used to significantly reduce the number of runs necessary to fit a DBN to simulated data. In the first paper (Chapter 4), we supplemented simulated data with bootstrapped data reducing the required number of runs for a single design point from 10,000 points to 1,500. Bootstrapping 1,500 simulation runs up to 10,000 data points produced DBNs that were significantly similar to ground truth DBNs built from 10,000 individually simulated data points. This 2-sample Kolmgorov-Smirnov (KS) test was used to make this comparison. Data bootstrapped from 1,500 simulated data points ensured that approximately 95% of the variables under consideration in the DBN would pass the KS test when compared to their counterparts in the "ground-truth" DBN. This percentage of acceptance increases to over 99% when the bootstrap sample size is increased to 3,000, however, at a bootstrap sample size of 750 this percentage is approximately 83%. Through bootstrapping we have reduced the number of simulation runs necessary to fit a DBN to simulated data by 85% and arguably by 92.5% depending upon the resolution required in the decision makers model.

Next, we explored various experimental designs coupled with bootstrapping to reduce the number of simulation runs needed even more and to cover the input parameter space of the DBN. We settled on a 12 run Maximum-Entropy Space Filling Design to span the space and again used the KS test as well as our interpolation technique to compare the results from bootstrapping and the space filling design. The results indicated that we can produce a significant DBN with 68% interpolation success by bootstrapping 500 data points strategically simulated across the design space at a significant level of 0.01. Interpolation coverage can be increased to approximately 80% when we increase the bootstrap sample size from 500 to 1,100. Experimental Designs and bootstrapping can reduce the necessary number of simulated data points by 89 - 95% with good interpolation coverage.

A major drawback to DBNs is that they discretize the data being modeled. This has one of two effects: either there are gaps in the model where the bins of the disretized data do not intersect or the bins are connected by assuming a uniform distribution over the data between each bin, which may be an incorrect assumption. To handle data between the defined bins in the DBN interpolation techniques were explored. This work, through Linear Regression, produced an interpolation technique that improves the interpolation coverage of the current methods by almost 44% for a bootstrap sample size of 500. This coverage is increased by 53.7% when the bootstrap sample size is increased to 1,100.

The primary focus of this research was to make DBN metamodeling for combat models a feasible goal. The final work that contributed to this goal was a case study (Chapter 6) that successfully fit a DBN to a mission level combat model. The results indicated that a DBN could be used to metamodel simulated data from a combat model using 3,000 simulation runs when comparing to a "ground-truth" DBN using the KS test. However, the interpolation results were very good even without bootstrapping, indicating that the probability output space of the DBN is very linear with small variability in the combat model. Therefore, depending on the level of resolution required by the decision maker it is possible to fit a useful DBN to a combat model with a very small number of simulation runs.

The next two contributions do not apply directly to the goal of the research, but are results of the research conducted. Two novel applications of bootstrapping are developed in this research. Typically bootstrapping is used to estimate the statistics of interest concerning a large data set or distribution when only a small sample set is available. This work proposes that bootstrapping can also generate new data to be used in conjunction with the original sample.

Finally, in introducing DBNs as suitable metamodels for combat models as well as Modeling and Simulation in general, it was necessary to do a thorough review of the M&S analysis process. In this review we introduce the start of and argue for a standard M&S framework that can be easily understood for the analyst. This framework gives a chartable overview of the output and input analysis pieces of M&S. The framework names many common practice techniques and where they should be applied in the process. This framework does not require the analyst to limit himself to the techniques and outline proposed, but provide a starting point with check along the way to ensure proper steps are being taken. Also, the framework will allow for translatable results so that analysts can effectively understand the models and results of others in their community.

7.2 Future Research

Though this research has produced practical contributions that can be applied in the M&S world, it has also fostered many questions and future research opportunities.

The lower bound derived by Poropudas in Equation 4.2 is a power test. The analyst determines the variables for Equation 4.2 which then returns a minimum number of experimental observations necessary to fit a DBN to the data. Future work should look to determine a more robust lower bound that is not as dependent upon the analysts input. The lower bound might instead depend upon the number of variables present in the model or some combination of the number of variables present and the number of discredited bins for each variable.

When comparing the bootstrapped DBNs and "ground-truth" DBNs in this research the major factor under consideration was the bootstrap sample size, b. More work should be done to done to understand the relationship between the number of simulation runs necessary to fit a DBN, N, the bootstrap sample size and the significance level, α for the Confidence Intervals used to test interpolation, Equation **??**. For example, Figures 43 - 45 plot the interpolation coverage results for various bootstrap sample sizes, "ground-truth" sample sizes and α levels. Can we determine the closed form relationship or approximate a relationship between the number of runs necessary to fit a DBN and bootstrap sample size?

There are many other future research areas present in this work. The techniques developed in this dissertation should be applied to and tested on a larger campaign

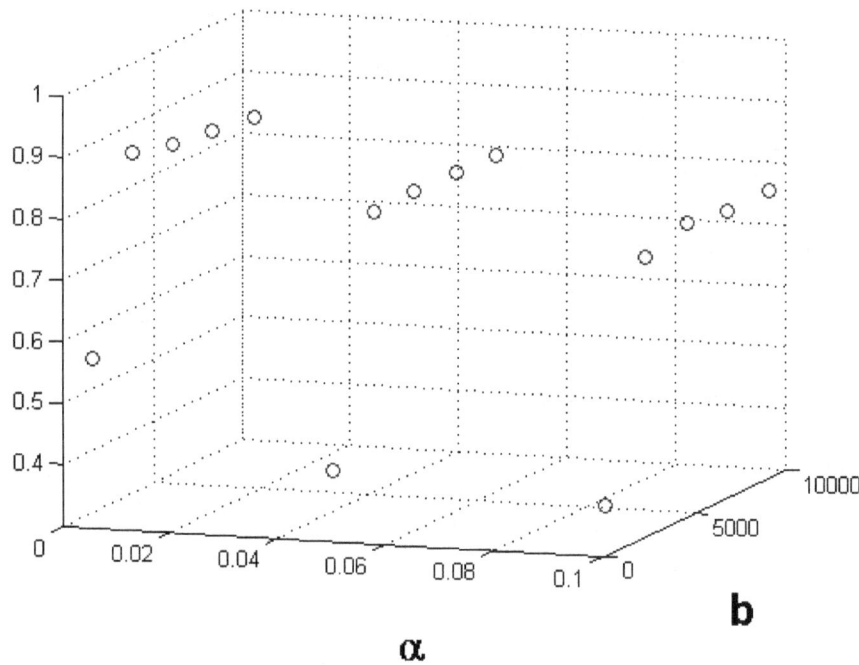

Figure 43. Rock curve for interpolation coverage over various bootstrap sample sizes and α levels.

level combat model. Six experimental designs were considered, but there are many more that should be explored. A very basic bootstrapping technique was utilized in this research, but more sophisticated methods exist that might improve the results. A goodness of fit test using the Kullback-Leibler Divergence was proposed in the first paper, but still needs to be developed and tested. DBNs as metamodels might be extended and improved by combining this work with DBNs built from subject matter experts and DBNs built from observed or historical data. There is a wealth of research opportunities here that could add value to the M&S community and improve the use of DBNs as metamodels.

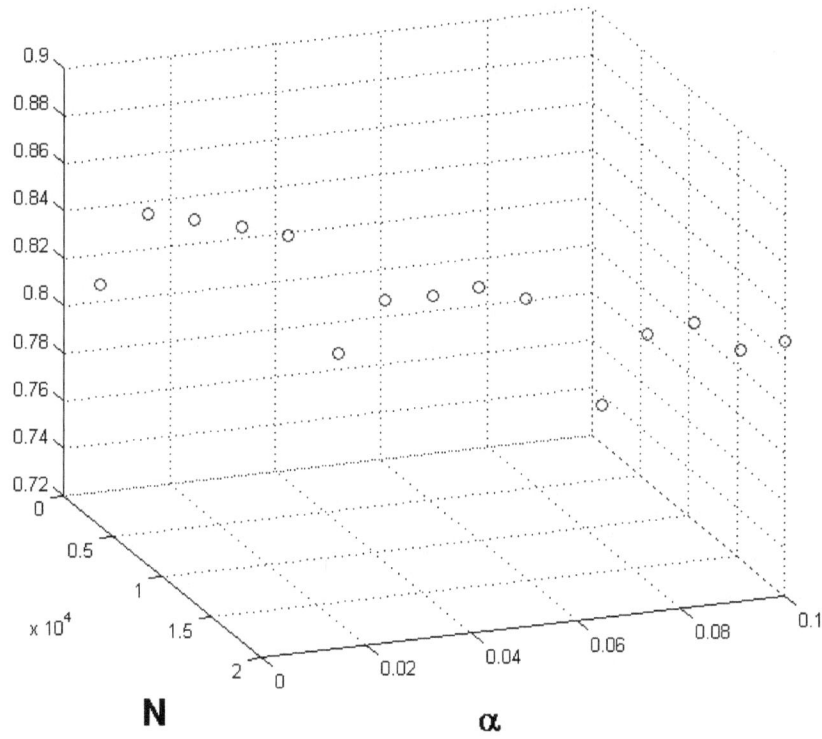

Figure 44. Rock curve for interpolation coverage over various sample sizes for necessary number of simulation runs and α levels.

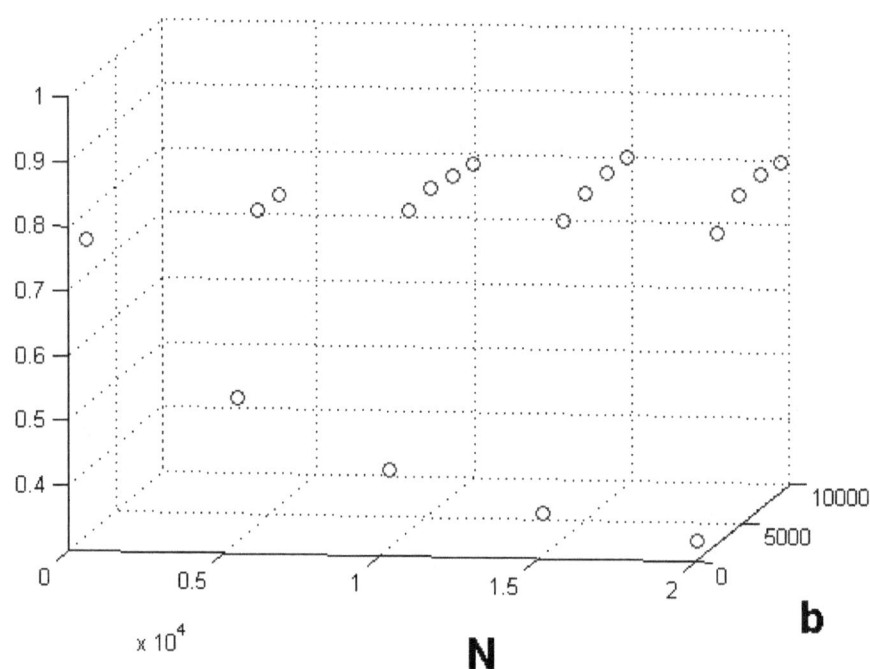

Figure 45. Rock curve for interpolation coverage over various various sample sizes for necessary number of simulation runs and bootstrap sample sizes.

Bibliography

[1] Anderson, Theodore W and Donald A Darling. "A test of goodness of fit", *Journal of the American Statistical Association*, 49(268):765–769, 1954.

[2] Boutilier, Craig, Nir Friedman, Moises Goldszmidt, and Daphne Koller. "Context-specific independence in Bayesian networks". *Proceedings of the Twelfth international conference on Uncertainty in artificial intelligence*, 115–123. Morgan Kaufmann Publishers Inc., 1996.

[3] Caffrey Jr, Matthew. *Toward a history-based doctrine for wargaming*. Technical report, DTIC Document, 2000.

[4] Champagne, Lance E. *Development approaches coupled with verification and validation methodologies for agent-based mission-level analytical combat simulations*. Ph.D. thesis, Air Force Institute of Technology, WPAFB, Oh, 2004.

[5] Chang, Kuo-Chu and Robert Fung. "Refinement and coarsening of Bayesian networks", *arXiv preprint arXiv:1304.1138*, 2013.

[6] Chen, Serena H and Carmel A Pollino. "Good practice in Bayesian network modelling", *Environmental Modelling & Software*, 2012.

[7] Darling, Donald A. "The kolmogorov-smirnov, cramer-von mises tests", *The Annals of Mathematical Statistics*, 823–838, 1957.

[8] Darwiche, Adnan. *Modeling and reasoning with Bayesian networks*, volume 1. Cambridge University Press Cambridge, 2009.

[9] Davis, P.K. and D. Blumenthal. *The base of sand problem: A white paper on the state of military combat modeling*. Technical report, DTIC Document, 1991.

[10] Druzdel, MJ and Linda C Van Der Gaag. "Building probabilistic networks:" Where do the numbers come from?"", *IEEE Transactions on knowledge and data engineering*, 12(4):481–486, 2000.

[11] Efron, Bradley. "Bootstrap methods: another look at the jackknife", *The Annals of Statistics*, 78:1–26, 1979.

[12] Efron, Bradley. *The jackknife, the bootstrap and other resampling plans*. SIAM, 1982.

[13] Efron, Bradley and Robert J Tibshirani. *An introduction to the bootstrap*, volume 57. CRC press, 1994.

[14] ExoAnalytic Solutions, Inc. "TeamSEAS homepage", July 2014. URL `https://www.teamseas.com/`.

[15] Flores, M Julia, José A Gámez, and Kristian G Olesen. "Incremental compilation of Bayesian networks". *Proceedings of the Nineteenth conference on Uncertainty in Artificial Intelligence*, 233–240. Morgan Kaufmann Publishers Inc., 2002.

[16] Friedman, Linda Weiser and Hershey H Friedman. "The probability distribution as a performance criterion when comparing alternative systems", *Simulation*, 45(5):262–264, 1985.

[17] Gallagher, Dr. Mark. *Defense Forces Exploration and Analysis Tool (DeFEAT)*. Technical report, AF/A9, August 2012.

[18] Grzegorczyk, Marco and Dirk Husmeier. "Non-stationary continuous dynamic Bayesian networks", 2009.

[19] Halpern, J.Y. *Reasoning about uncertainty*. MIT Press, 2003.

[20] Hulten, Geoff, David Maxwell Chickering, and David Heckerman. "Learning Bayesian networks from dependency networks: a preliminary study". *Proceedings of the Ninth International Workshop on Artificial Intelligence and Statistics*. 2003.

[21] Jensen, Finn Verner and Thomas Dyhre Nielsen. *Bayesian networks and decision graphs*. Springer, 2007.

[22] JMP. "Space-Filling Designs", June 2014. URL http://www.jmp.com/support/help/Space-Filling_Designs.shtml.

[23] Johnson, Rachel Terese. *The Design and Analysis of Computer Experiments*. Ph.D. thesis, Arizona State University, 2008.

[24] Kelleher, Clayton T, Raymond R Hill, and Kenneth W Bauer. "Fitting Dynamic Bayesian Networks to Simulated Data with Bootstrapping", 2014.

[25] Kelleher, Clayton T, Raymond R Hill, and Kenneth W Bauer. "Using Experimental Deisgn and Interpolatin Methods for Dynamic Bayesian Network Metamodeling", 2014.

[26] Kjaerulff, Uffe B and Anders L Madsen. *Bayesian networks and influence diagrams: a guide to construction and analysis*, volume 22. Springer, 2013.

[27] Kleijnen, Jack PC, Sudsan M Sanchez, Thomas W Lucas, and Thomas M Cioppa. "A User's Guide to the Brave New World of Designing Simulation Experiments", *Journal on Computing*, 17(3):263–289, 2005.

[28] Koski, Timo and John Noble. *Bayesian networks: an introduction*, volume 924. Wiley, 2011.

[29] Kutner, Michael H, Christopher J Nachtsheim, John Neter, and William Li. "Applied linear statistical models", 2005.

[30] Li, Ying, RS Singii, and YG Sun. "Goodness-of-fit tests of a parameric density functions: monte carlo simulation studies", *Journal of Statistical Research*, 39(2):111–133, 2005.

[31] Liao, Wenhui and Qiang Ji. "Learning Bayesian network parameters under incomplete data with domain knowledge", *Pattern Recognition*, 42(11):3046–3056, 2009.

[32] Mahoney, Suzanne M. "Introduction to Bayesian Networks using NETICA Training". Innovative Decisions, Inc., 2013.

[33] Merriam-Webster. "Merriam-Webster Online Dictionary", January 2013. URL http://www.merriam-webster.com/info/copyright.htm.

[34] Merriam-Webster. "Software Packages for Graphical Models", February 2013. URL http://people.cs.ubc.ca/~murphyk/Software/bnsoft.html.

[35] Miller, J O. "OPER 671 - Joint Combat Modeling I". University Project, 2013.

[36] Minsky, Marvin. "Steps toward artificial intelligence", *Computers and thought*, 406:450, 1963.

[37] Murphy, Kevin Patrick. *Dynamic bayesian networks: representation, inference and learning*. Ph.D. thesis, University of California, 2002.

[38] Myers, Raymond H, Douglas C Montgomery, and Christine M Anderson-Cook. *Response surface methodology: process and product optimization using designed experiments*, third edition). John Wiley & Sons, 2009.

[39] Neapolitan, Richard E. *Probabilistic Reasoning in Expert Systems: Theory and Algorithms*. John Wiley & Sons, Inc., 1989.

[40] Neapolitan, Richard E. *Learning bayesian networks*. Pearson Prentice Hall Upper Saddle River, 2004.

[41] Pearl, Judea. *Bayesian Networks: a model of self-activated: memory for evidential reasoning*. Computer Science Department, University of California, 1985.

[42] Pearl, Judea. "Fusion, propagation, and structuring in belief networks", *Artificial intelligence*, 29(3):241–288, 1986.

[43] Pearl, Judea. *Probabilistic Reasoning in Intelligent Systems: Networks of Plausble Inference*. Morgan Kaufmann Pub, 1988.

[44] Peng, Yun and Zhongli Ding. "Modifying Bayesian networks by probability constraints", *arXiv preprint arXiv:1207.1356*, 2012.

[45] Peng, Yun, Shenyong Zhang, and Rong Pan. "Bayesian network reasoning with uncertain evidences", *International Journal of Uncertainty, Fuzziness and Knowledge-Based Systems*, 18(05):539–564, 2010.

[46] Pettitt, Ao No. "A two-sample Anderson-Darling rank statistic", *Biometrika*, 63(1):161–168, 1976.

[47] Poropudas, Jirka and Kai Virtanen. "Analyzing air combat simulation results with dynamic Bayesian networks". *Proceedings of the 39th conference on Winter simulation: 40 years! The best is yet to come*, 1370–1377. IEEE Press, 2007.

[48] Poropudas, Jirka and Kai Virtanen. "Simulation metamodeling in continuous time using dynamic Bayesian networks". *Proceedings of the Winter Simulation Conference*, 935–946. Winter Simulation Conference, 2010.

[49] Poropudas, Jirka and Kai Virtanen. "Simulation metamodeling with dynamic Bayesian networks", *European Journal of Operational Research*, 214(3):644–655, 2011.

[50] Pourret, Olivier, Patrick Naïm, and Bruce Marcot. *Bayesian networks: a practical guide to applications*, volume 73. Wiley, 2008.

[51] Pousi, J., J. Poropudas, and K. Virtanen. "Simulation metamodelling with Bayesian networks", *J Simulation*, 7(4):297–311, Nov 2013. ISSN 1747-7778. URL http://dx.doi.org/10.1057/jos.2013.18.

[52] Pousi, Jouni, Jirka Poropudas, and Kai Virtanen. "Simulation metamodelling with bayesian networks", *Journal of Simulation*, 7(4):297–311, 2013.

[53] Robinson, Joshua W and Alexander J Hartemink. "Non-stationary dynamic Bayesian networks". *Advances in Neural Information Processing Systems*, 1369–1376. 2008.

[54] Scholz, FW and MA Stephens. "K-sample Anderson–Darling tests", *Journal of the American Statistical Association*, 82(399):918–924, 1987.

[55] Scutari, Marco. "Learning Bayesian networks with the bnlearn R package", *arXiv preprint arXiv:0908.3817*, 2009.

[56] Seila, A.F. "The case for a standard model description for process simulation", *International Journal of Simulation and Process Modelling*, 1(1):26–34, 2005.

[57] Sierra, B, E Lazkano, E Jauregi, and I Irigoien. "Histogram distance-based Bayesian Network structure learning: A supervised classification specific approach", *Decision Support Systems*, 48(1):180–190, 2009.

[58] Song, Kai-Sheng. "Goodness-of-fit tests based on Kullback-Leibler discrimination information", *IEEE Transactions on Information Theory*, 48(5):1103–1117, 2002.

[59] Spirtes, Peter. "Directed cyclic graphical representations of feedback models". *Proceedings of the Eleventh Conference on Uncertainty in Artificial Intelligence*, 491–498. Morgan Kaufmann Publishers Inc., 1995.

[60] Tolk, Andreas. *Engineering principles of combat modeling and distributed simulation*. Wiley, 2012.

[61] Tulupyev, Alexander L and Sergey I Nikolenko. "Directed cycles in bayesian belief networks: probabilistic semantics and consistency checking complexity". *MICAI 2005: Advances in Artificial Intelligence*, 214–223. Springer, 2005.

[62] Uusitalo, Laura. "Advantages and challenges of Bayesian networks in environmental modelling", *Ecological modelling*, 203(3):312–318, 2007.

[63] Wehrens, Ron, Hein Putter, and Lutgarde Buydens. "The bootstrap: a tutorial", *Chemometrics and intelligent laboratory systems*, 54(1):35–52, 2000.

[64] Withers, B.D., A.A.B. Pritsker, and D.H. Withers. "A structured definition of the modeling process". *Proceedings of the 25th conference on Winter simulation*, 1109–1117. IEEE, 1993.

[65] Wright, Sewall. "The theory of path coefficients a reply to Niles's criticism", *Genetics*, 8(3):239, 1923.

[66] Wright, Sewall. "The method of path coefficients", *The Annals of Mathematical Statistics*, 5(3):161–215, 1934.

[67] Wu, CF Jeff and Michael S Hamada. *Experiments: Planning, Analysis and Optimization, Hoboken*, second edition). John Wiley & Sons, Hoboken, New Jersey, 2009.

www.ingramcontent.com/pod-product-compliance
Lightning Source LLC
Chambersburg PA
CBHW081221280526
45787CB00006B/2475

* 9 7 8 1 5 0 7 5 6 3 0 4 5 *